READY**SET** CROCHET

LEARN TO CROCHET WITH **19** HOT PROJECTS

SUSIE JOHNS

Creative Publishing
international

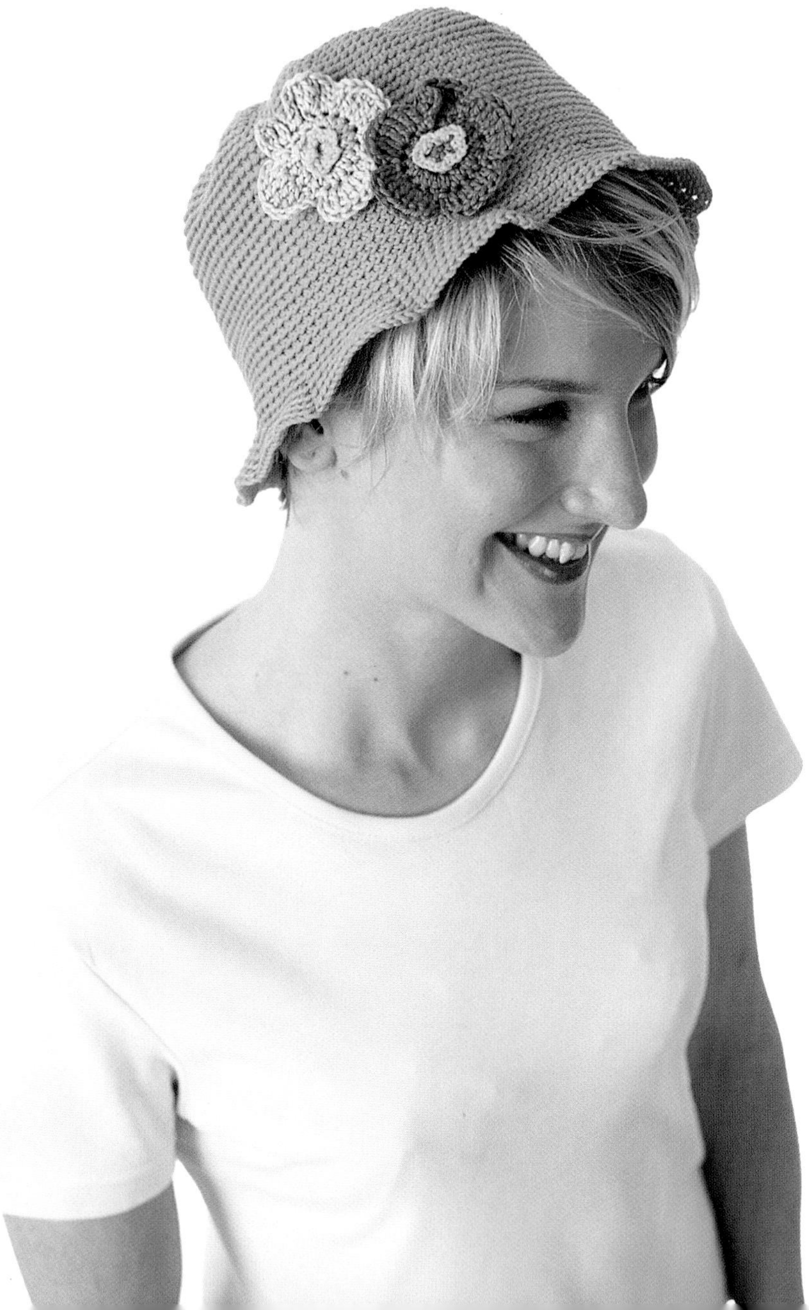

First published in 2004 in the USA and Canada by Creative Publishing international, Inc.

Creative Publishing
international

18705 Lake Drive East
Chanhassen Minnesota 55317
1-800-328-3895
www.creativepub.com

President/CEO: Ken Fund
Vice President/Publisher: Linda Ball
Vice President/Retail Sales: Kevin Haas
Executive Editor/Lifestyles: Alison Brown Cerier

First published in UK in 2004 by
Carroll & Brown Publishers
20 Lonsdale Road
Queens Park
London NW6 6RD

Project Editor: Caroline Smith
Managing Art Editor: Emily Cook
Photographer: Jules Selmes

ISBN 1-58923-186-4

Reproduced by RDC, Malaysia
Printed by Tien Wah Press, Singapore

10 9 8 7 6 5 4 3

CONTENTS

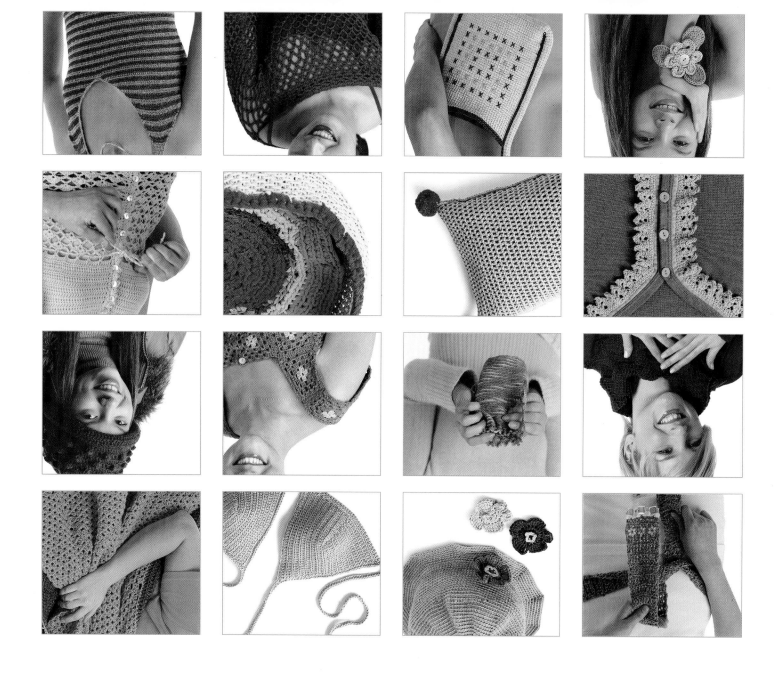

INTRODUCTION

Ready, set, crochet! One of the most versatile of handicrafts, crochet is easy to learn, simple to do, and requires very little in the way of materials—just a hook and a ball of yarn.

Crochet's charm lies in its simplicity: there are very few basic stitches to learn but they can be combined to create an almost infinite variety of patterns and textures. Used imaginatively, crochet can create a fabric that is firm and hard-edged, one that is soft and flexible, one that is intricate and detailed, or one that is light, open, and delicate. Crochet can be worked in rows or in the round, to form not only flat fabrics but shaped and contoured ones, too. Many crocheted items can be worked in one piece—so there's no sewing up and no bulky seams.

Crochet is also quick! Most of the patterns in this book could be completed in a few sessions. Buy the hook and yarn today and you could be wearing your own hand-made hat, scarf, or bikini top in a matter of days.

This book starts you off with a few fundamentals: the basic stitches, the best working practices, and the techniques you'll need to shape your crochet. Two quick and simple patterns follow: a pretty bikini top and a fabulous funky belt, both of which you can easily make in a couple of evenings.

By manipulating those basic stitches, you can give your crochet new texture and interest. Using different colored yarns will also add a new element to your crochet. You'll find information here on changing colors and using graphs, followed by a pattern for a stylish striped top. More variations on the basic techniques follow, along with patterns that put the methods you have learned into practice.

Crochet pieces are often worked in the round. You'll find a simple explanation of the basic technique and how it is adapted to create some stunning shapes as well as practical clothes and bags. A section on raised patterns follows, showing you just how versatile crochet can be as you create cables, bobbles, and bullion stitches.

Part of crochet's traditional appeal lies in the lacy, open look that can be achieved.

Here, you'll find information on how to create this kind of work, from simple picot edgings to delicate filet crochet. As with all the techniques described in this book, you'll find plenty of patterns that give you the chance to use your new found skills. Patterns that, hopefully, will inspire you to take up this exciting, but age-old, handicraft.

Although crochet is a traditional craft, it certainly isn't stuck in the past. Every year new designers discover its unique appeal. New stitch patterns are invented, new garments are produced, and another generation is encouraged to learn the simple skills required for this creative craft.

You'll also find that there's an inspiring range of different yarns available to use in your work—from traditional crochet cottons to multi-hued novelty yarns. And you don't have to stop there. Try using string. Dye your own yarn. Try leather lacing, ribbons, or strips of fabric, either cut or torn. Add beads, buttons, or appliqué, and combine crochet with knitting. The possibilities, as the saying goes, are limited only by your imagination.

As more and more people appreciate hand-made textiles and the value of traditional crafts, crochet, now more than ever, has so much to offer. I hope this book gets you hooked!

HOOKS AND YARNS

Crochet hooks come in different sizes and materials. There are fine steel hooks and larger ones made of aluminum, plastic, or wood. Yarns are sold by weight and/or length. Beginners will find it helpful to choose a smooth yarn in a heavy weight that is not likely to untwist while you work. Generally, the coarser the yarn, the larger the hook you will need.

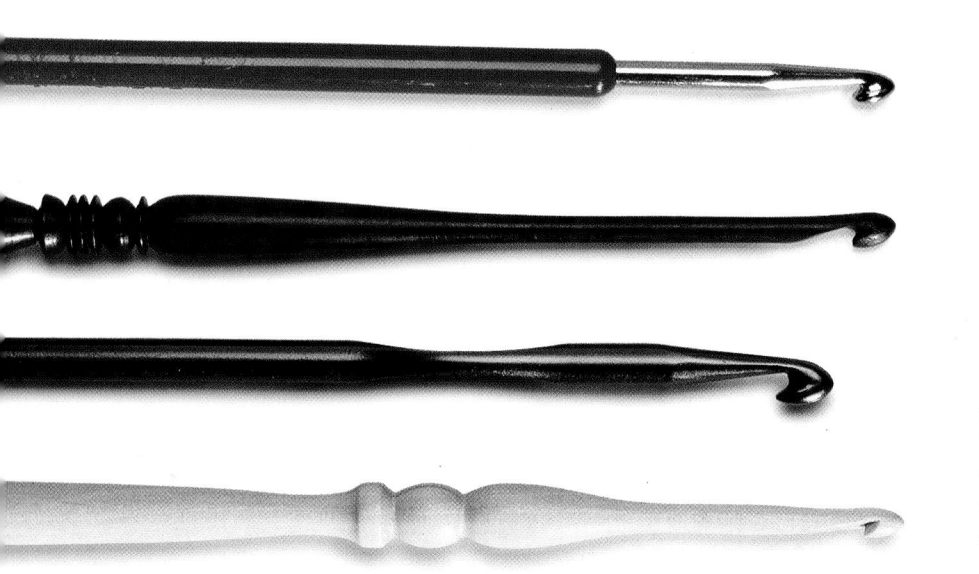

HOOKS

Crochet hooks are labeled in several ways—a letter, number, and/or a metric measurement. Steel and aluminum hooks come in a large range of sizes, but wooden hooks are also popular. Avoid cheaper plastic versions that may have rough edges. Afghan crochet needs a very long hook (shown at the bottom here) that has a knob at the end, similar to that on a knitting needle, or another hook.

Sometimes a hook size is given on the yarn's label: use this as a starting point to obtain the gauge (see pages 18–19). Novelty yarns can be worked with a larger hook than a smooth yarn of similar weight. If you are mixing more than one yarn in a garment, check that they share the same care instructions.

CROCHET HOOK SIZES

US sizes			Metric sizes
Size	B	=	2 mm
Size	1	=	2.25 mm
Size	C	=	2.5 mm
Size	2	=	2.75 mm
Size	D	=	3 mm
Size	3	=	3.25 mm
Size	E	=	3.5 mm
Size	4	=	3.5 mm
Size	5	=	3.75 mm
Size	F	=	4 mm
Size	6	=	4.25 mm
Size	G	=	4.5 mm
Size	7	=	4.5 mm
Size	H	=	5 mm
Size	8	=	5 mm
Size	I	=	5.5 mm
Size	9	=	5.5 mm
Size	J	=	6 mm
Size	10	=	6 mm
Size	10½	=	6.5 mm
Size	K	=	7 mm
Size	11	=	8 mm
Size	13	=	9 mm
Size	15	=	10 mm
Steel hooks			
Size	0	=	2.5 mm
Size	1	=	2 mm
Size	4	=	1.75 mm
Size	6	=	1.5 mm
Size	10	=	1 mm
Size	12	=	0.75 mm

YARNS

There are standard terms for the most popular weights of yarns. These yarns may be made of different numbers of strands spun together; 2-, 3- and 4-ply are all common. Fine weight is usually used for lace work and edgings. It is half or less as thick as fingering weight. Fingering weight, for delicate garments and baby items, is often a 3-ply yarn. Sport weight, the middle of the weight range, is for sweaters, cardigans, or afghans. Knitting worsted is for chunkier jackets and sweaters, and is equivalent to two strands of sport weight. Fisherman (Aran) weight is equivalent to three strands of sport weight, and is used for heavy afghans or jackets. Bulky weight, for warm outdoor garments, is equivalent to four strands of sport weight or two strands of knitting worsted.

BEGINNING TO CROCHET

Crochet work, like knitting, is created from a continuous length of yarn.

In crochet a single hook is used to work one stitch at a time.

You start with a slip knot then continue to make loops (called chains) to

form a foundation chain from which you make the first row.

LEFT-HANDED CROCHETERS

If you are left-handed, hold the working yarn in your right hand and hold the hook in the left hand.

Before you get started, it's a good idea to become comfortable with holding the hook and yarn. You can hold them any way you like, as long as you can work freely and your hands don't feel cramped. Here, we show the two most common ways of holding the hook but you could devise a method to suit yourself.

The two most common methods of controlling yarn are also shown here. The way you hold yarn does have an important part to play—the yarn tension is controlled with your middle finger or forefinger. As you crochet, you want to be able to control the yarn evenly and work uniform chains, so practice the different methods to find which one is easiest for you.

HOLDING THE HOOK

Both methods are equally good, so use whichever feels most comfortable.

Pencil position
Grasp the flat part of the hook between thumb and forefinger as if it were a pencil with the stem above your hand.

Knife position
With the stem against your palm and your thumb on the flat part, grasp the hook between thumb and fingers.

PENCIL POSITION
Hold the hook as if it were a pencil.

KNIFE POSITION
Hold the hook as if you were using a knife.

MAKING A SLIP KNOT

To begin crochet you need to make a slip knot. About 6 inches (15 cm) from the yarn end, make a loop. Insert the hook and catch the working yarn, drawing it up through the loop. Pull both ends to tighten the knot and then slide it up to the hook.

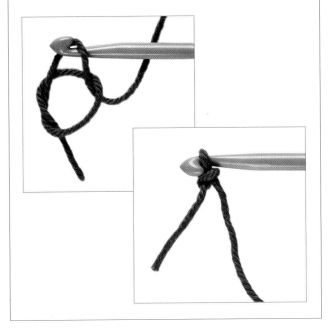

CONTROLLING THE YARN

The way you hold the yarn allows it to flow easily with the right tension. You can wrap the yarn around your little finger, over the next two fingers, and catch it with your forefinger—when your middle finger will control the yarn. Or you can wrap the yarn around your little finger, then under your next two fingers and over your forefinger—when your forefinger will control the yarn. With thick yarn, you can catch it between your fourth and fifth fingers. Use the method that feels most comfortable.

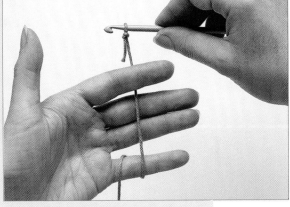

FOREFINGER METHOD

Pass the working yarn around the little finger, under the next two fingers and over the forefinger (*top*). With the hook through the slip loop, and holding the slip knot between thumb and middle finger of the left hand, prepare to make the first chain by raising your forefinger.

MIDDLE FINGER METHOD

Pass the working yarn around the little finger, and over the other fingers (*right*). With the hook through the slip loop, and holding the slip knot between the thumb and forefinger of the left hand, prepare to make the first chain by raising your middle finger.

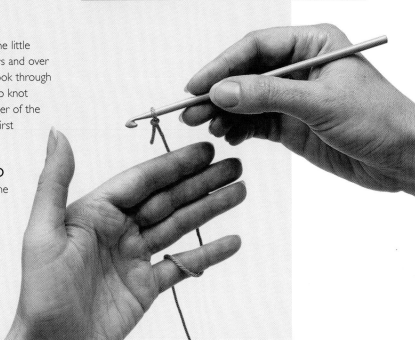

FOUNDATION STITCHES

The first row of a piece of crochet is called the foundation chain. It may be short—just one or two stitches—or it may be quite long. This chain is the base for the remaining work and needs to be neat and even.

Your work begins with a good foundation chain—and further chains can be put to good use to make simple cords and ties (see pages 58–59).

COUNTING CHAINS

Each chain (loop) counts as one stitch. To count the chains correctly, make sure that they are not twisted and that the fronts are facing you. The loop currently on the hook is never counted as a stitch, nor is the slip knot at the beginning of the foundation chain. There is always one loop left on the hook after completing every stitch, and this is referred to as the working loop.

Once you've made yourself comfortable with your hook and yarn and formed your first slip knot (see pages 8–9), you are ready to make a foundation chain. Chain stitch (abbreviated to *ch*) is usually used. This is simply made by pulling the yarn through the slip knot and then each subsequent loop on the hook. Chain stitch is also used as part of a pattern stitch, to make spaces between stitches, for bars in openwork (see page 77), and for the turning chains at the beginnings of rows/rounds (see pages 16 and 53). The length of the foundation chain will be specified in the pattern instruction.

Slip stitch (abbreviated to *sl st*) is the most basic of crochet stitches—some of the earliest crochet work found was done in continuous slip stitch—and is made by simply drawing the yarn through the work and the loop on the hook at the same time. Today, slip stitch is used most commonly to join a row into a round (see page 53), to decrease (see page 22), and for joining seams (see pages 26–27), although you will find it used occasionally for a variety of patterns.

FOUNDATION CHAIN

The foundation chain should be worked loosely and evenly to ensure that the hook can enter each loop easily on the first row. The hook and your tension will determine the size of the chains. Do not try to make chains loose by pulling them as you make them, since this tightens up previously made chains. If the chains are too tight, ensure that the yarn is flowing through your fingers easily, or use a larger hook than you will use for the rest of your work. The length of the foundation chain will be specified in the pattern instruction.

MAKING A
CHAIN STITCH (ch)

1. Hold the hook in your right hand. Keeping the working yarn taut, grasp the slip knot with the thumb and middle finger of your left hand. Push the hook forward and take the hook under (anti-clockwise), behind and then over the yarn, so that the yarn passes round the hook and is caught in it. This is called a yarn-over—or yo.

2. Draw the hook and yarn back through the slip loop to form the first chain stitch.

3. Repeat steps 1 and 2. After making a few chains in this way, move your left hand up so that you are holding the work directly under the hook for maximum control, and continue.

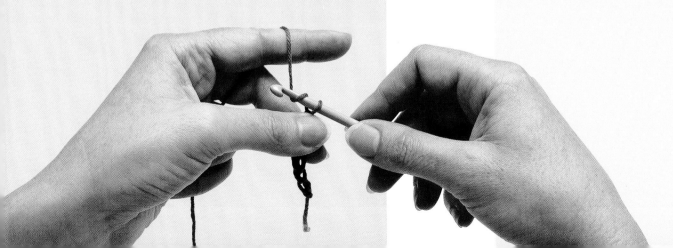

MAKING A
SLIP STITCH (sl st)

1. Make a length of evenly worked foundation chain.

2. Insert the hook from front to back under the top of the second chain (ch) from the hook. Wrap the yarn around the hook to make a yarn-over (yo).

3. Draw the yarn through the two loops now on the hook, making a slip stitch. To continue working slip stitch, insert the hook into the next and each chain, and repeat step 2 as required.

BASIC STITCHES

It is easy to learn crochet stitches because they are all made the same way. Apart from the chain and the slip stitch, there are five basic crochet stitches, which vary in height (there are others, but these tend to be more advanced and are used less frequently).

The difference in the height or length of these stitches is determined by the number of times the yarn is wrapped around the hook. As each stitch has a flatter appearance on the front than on the back, the crocheted piece has more texture when worked in rows and turned because you see both the fronts and the backs of the stitches. The surface has a smoother, flatter look when worked in rows/rounds without turning, as it always shows the front of the stitches.

✤ DOUBLE CROCHET (dc) (see page 15)

Twice as high as single crochet, this stitch works up quickly. It is the most commonly used stitch.

✤ HALF DOUBLE CROCHET (hdc)

Between single and double crochet in size, this stitch produces a slightly looser surface with an attractive ridge.

✤ SINGLE CROCHET (sc)

This simple compact stitch (left) is found in many pattern designs and forms a firm, smooth surface.

SINGLE CROCHET (sc)

1. Make a foundation chain. Skip 2 chains (chs) and insert the hook under top loop of 3rd chain (ch).

2. Wrap the yarn over the hook (yo) and draw it through the ch loop only.

3. There are 2 loops on the hook. Yo (see step 2) and draw the yarn through both loops. Single crochet (sc) made.

4. Continue working sc into the next and all following chs to the end of the row.

5. To make next and following rows of sc, turn work and ch 1. This is called the turning chain (t-ch) and counts as first sc in new row. Skip the first stitch (st), at base of t-ch, work 1 sc into top 2 loops of 2nd st in previous row. Work 1 sc into next and each st to end, including top of t-ch.

HALF DOUBLE CROCHET (hdc)

1. Make a foundation chain. Skip 2 chs, yo and insert the hook under top loop of 3rd ch, yo.

2. Draw the yarn through the ch loop only (there are 3 loops on hook), yo.

3. Draw the yarn through all 3 loops. Half double crochet (hdc) made. Continue working hdc into next and all following chs to end of the row.

4. To make next and following rows of hdc, turn work and ch 2. This is the t-ch and counts as first hdc in new row. Skip the first st at base of t-ch, work 1 hdc into top 2 loops of 2nd st in previous row. Work 1 hdc into next and each st to end, including top of t-ch.

MORE BASIC STITCHES

Whenever you are working the basic stitches, shown here and on page 12, onto the foundation chain, insert the hook from front to back under the top loop of each chain. On subsequent rows, unless instructed otherwise, insert your hook from front to back under the top two loops of each stitch.

At the end of each row, turn the work then make extra chains, called turning chains, to bring the hook level with the height of the stitches in the new row (see pages 16–17). The turning chains may or may not count as stitches at the beginning of a row, according to the pattern. They do count as stitches in the basic stitch patterns shown on pages 13 and 15.

❖ **DOUBLE TRIPLE CROCHET (dtr)**

This extremely long stitch is used in fancy stitch patterns, but is not generally used continuously to make a whole piece, except where it is linked (see page 33).

❖ **TRIPLE CROCHET (tr)**

Three times as high as single crochet, this stitch (left) forms an open, looser texture.

DOUBLE CROCHET (dc)

1. Make a foundation chain. Skip 3 chs, yo and insert the hook under the top loop of 4th ch, yo.

2. Draw the yarn through the ch loop only (there are 3 loops on the hook), yo.

3. Draw the yarn through 2 loops only (2 loops on hook), yo.

4. Draw the yarn through these 2 loops. Double crochet (dc) made. Continue working dc into next and all following chs to end of the row. To make next and following rows of dc, turn work and ch 3. This is the t-ch and counts as first dc in new row. Skip the first st at base of t-ch, work 1 dc into top 2 loops of 2nd st in previous row. Work 1 dc into next and each st to end, including into top of t-ch.

TRIPLE or TREBLE (tr)

1. Make a foundation chain. Skip 4 chs, yo 2 times and insert hook under top loop of 5th ch. Yo, draw yarn through ch loop only (4 loops on hook), yo.

2. Draw yarn through 2 loops only (3 loops on hook), yo. Draw yarn through 2 loops only, yo. Draw yarn through remaining 2 loops; triple (tr) made. Tr into next and following chs. To make next row of tr, turn work and ch 4. This t-ch counts as first tr in new row. Skip first st at base of t-ch. Work 1 tr, inserting hook under top 2 loops of 2nd st in previous row; continue.

DOUBLE TRIPLE (dtr)

1. Make a foundation chain. Skip 5 chs, yo 3 times and insert hook under top loop of 6th ch. Yo, draw yarn through ch loop only (5 loops on the hook), *Yo, draw yarn through 2 loops only.

2. Repeat from * three times more; double triple (dtr) made. Dtr into next and following chs. To make the next row, turn work and ch 5. This t-ch counts as first dtr in new row. Skip first st at base of t-ch. Work 1 dtr, inserting hook under top 2 loops of the 2nd st in previous row; continue.

WORKING PRACTICE

In crochet, there are some basic techniques to master and useful practices to follow that will help you as you work. Keep these methods in mind as you crochet and you'll get a neater finish.

TURNING CHAINS (t-ch)

To bring the hook up to the height of the stitches, you must add turning chains at the beginning of each row. Each of the basic stitches (see pages 12–15) has its own number of chains: the table below gives the numbers when the t-ch counts as the first stitch. Sometimes the t-ch may not be counted as a stitch (see Straight Edges, page 17). Some instructions say ch 2 and turn.

STITCH	Add to foundation chain	Skip at beginning of foundation row (counts as first st)	For turning chain counts as first st
Single	1	2	1
Half double	1	2	2
Double	2	3	3
Triple	3	4	4
Double triple	4	5	5

COUNTING STITCHES

To count short stitches, such as single crochet (as shown), it is easier to look at the tops. For longer stitches, count the upright stems —each is counted as a single stitch.

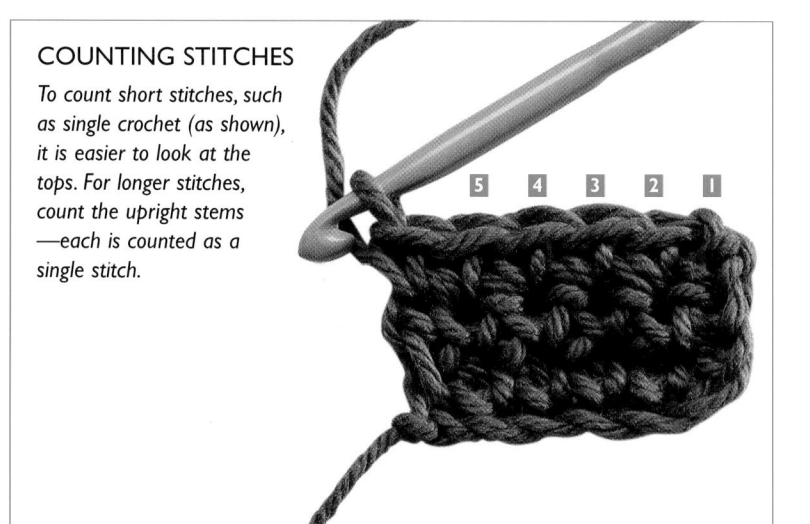

BINDING OFF

To prevent the work from raveling when you have finished, it is necessary to fasten the end. Complete the final stitch, then cut the working yarn and pull it through the last loop on the hook. Pull the yarn tight to close the loop. Thread the working end of the yarn into a tapestry or yarn needle and weave it into the back of the work.

WORKING IN ROWS

Crochet is normally worked in rows to produce the desired width, and the work is turned between each row. The right side of the work will not always be facing you.

1 *The first row is made by working across the foundation chain from right to left (if you are left-handed, work from left to right).*

2 *At the end of the foundation chain or row, turn the work so that the yarn is behind the hook and the new stitches can be worked into the tops of those in the previous row.*

STRAIGHT EDGES

To obtain straight edges and keep the number of stitches constant, you need to make the turning chains in one of two ways. The first is the most common, but the second is used with very short stitches, or to avoid the gap created by using the turning chain as a stitch. However, the second method creates slightly uneven edges.

TURNING CHAIN COUNTS AS FIRST STITCH

Skip the first stitch (st) of the previous row at the base of the turning chain (t-ch) (right). When you reach the end of the row (far right), work a st into the top of the t-ch of the previous row.

TURNING CHAIN DOES NOT COUNT AS STITCH

Work into the first st at the base of the t-ch (right). When you reach the end of the row (far right), do not work into the top of the previous t-ch.

GAUGE

The number of stitches and rows that are required to make a piece of crochet of a specific size depends upon four things: the yarn, the hook size, the stitch pattern, and the individual crocheter.

At the beginning of every crochet pattern you will find the stitch gauge. This indicates the number of stitches and rows in a particular measure, i.e. 15dc = 4" (15 double crochets = 4 inches)—and the entire design is based around this. To achieve the best results, you

must follow the stitch gauge. But since crochet is a true handcraft, each person's work will be slightly different. Before beginning a project, make a swatch to ensure that your tension matches that given. If you want to change the yarn or the stitch pattern, you can usually do so as long as you can still match the gauge.

MAKING ADJUSTMENTS

If, after making your sample, your gauge does not correspond with that given in the instructions, change to a bigger or smaller hook and crochet another sample.

Fewer stitches and rows than indicated means your work is too loose and you should try a smaller hook. More stitches and rows than shown means it is too tight and you should try a larger hook.

Occasionally you may find it impossible to match the gauge of both stitches and rows at the same time, in which case you should match the stitch gauge and compensate by working more or fewer rows, as necessary.

CHECKING THE GAUGE

Using the weight of yarn, hook size, and stitch pattern given with the instructions, crochet a sample at least 4 inches (10 cm) square. Place the finished sample right side up on a flat surface, taking care not to stretch it out of shape.

MEASURING STITCHES

Lay your ruler across the sample at the bottom of a row of stitches. Insert two pins vertically 4 inches (10 cm) apart. Count the number of stitches between the pins.

MEASURING ROWS

Now turn your ruler vertically and lay it along one side of a column of stitches. Avoiding the edges, place pins horizontally 4 inches (10 cm) apart. Count the rows between the pins.

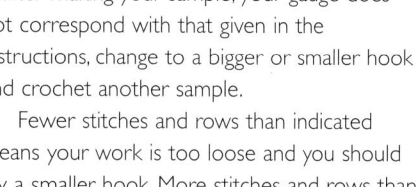
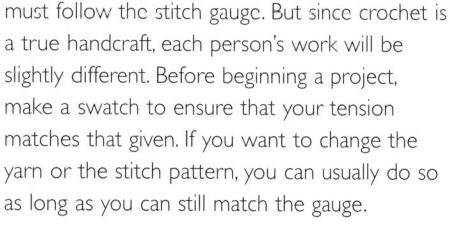

THE EFFECT OF YARNS AND PATTERNS

The weight of the yarn that you are using and the stitch pattern affect stitch gauge, so always work a sample before altering written instructions. Fine yarn will work with more stitches to the inch (2.5 cm) than heavier yarn, as will yarn worked with a smaller hook.

DIFFERENT YARNS

A thick yarn and a finer yarn worked on the same hook size and same stitch will result in different numbers of stitches per inch (2.5 cm).

DIFFERENT HOOK SIZES

The same yarn and stitch worked on different size hooks will work up to a different gauge.

DIFFERENT STITCHES

Different stitch patterns worked with the same hook and the same yarn will also produce different numbers of stitches per inch (2.5 cm).

INCREASING

Many crocheted items are made of simple squares or rectangles worked
evenly throughout to create a flat piece of work. There are times, however,
when it is necessary to shape your work by making it wider. This can be
done by increasing, that is by adding stitches.

There are many reasons why you might want to
add stitches to your crochet work. If you are
making a garment, you will want to fit it to the
shape of the body. Adding stitches at the right
place will make your work wider exactly where
it is needed.

Increasing while working in the round helps
add new elements to the pattern at the same
time as changing the shape of whatever you are
making. In fact, increases can be used to create
many decorative crochet patterns.

The easiest way to increase is to work twice
into one stitch (a single increase). You can do
this at the beginning and end of rows, to shape
the work at the sides, or across a row. If you
need to add more than two stitches, to make
multiple increases, you can do this at the
beginning and end of rows by working
additional chain stitches. This won't give you a
gradual shaping, the increase will form a definite
angle at the edge of the work.

*As you work this pretty summer hat, you increase
the stitches to help shape the crown (see page 56) .*

WORKING SINGLE INCREASES

When it is necessary to increase by a single stitch, the simplest way is to work twice into the same stitch. When you are making single increases one above another, across a row, work each subsequent pair into either the first or second of the previous pair consistently, so as to maintain lines of increase. To slant them to the right on a right side row, work each increase pair into the first of the previous pair; to slant them to the left, work them into the second.

AT THE BEGINNING OF A ROW

When the turning chain (t-ch) counts as a stitch (see pages 16–17): skip the first stitch (st) as usual and work 2 sts into the 2nd st, or work 1 st into the first st that you usually skip.

AT THE END OF A ROW

Work 2 sts into the last st (this will be the t-ch, if it counts as a st).

ACROSS A ROW

Pattern instructions usually tell you where to position each increase, but if not, spread them evenly across the row. Work 2 sts into the one below at each position.

MULTIPLE INCREASES

To increase by more than two stitches at the edge, make additional chain stitches. The method is the same for all the basic stitches. Here the turning chain counts as a stitch. When several stitches at once are made at an edge, a sharp angle is created.

AT THE BEGINNING OF A ROW

Add the the number of increases needed to the number of turning chains being used. For example, if you are working double crochet (dc), which needs 2 t-ch, and want to add 3 sts, you will need to chain (ch) 5 (left). Skip 3 ch (counts as 1 dc) and work 1 dc into each of the remaining 2 new chs, making 3 new sts, including t-ch (right).

AT THE END OF A ROW

To make the first additional increase st, insert the hook through the lower part of the last st made, picking up the single, vertical thread on its left-hand side (left). Continue inserting the hook into the base of the st just completed to work the required number of additional sts (right).

DECREASING

By decreasing, you can give crocheted garments form
and create openings, such as necklines and armholes.

It may be necessary to shape your crochet
work by subtracting stitches. These decreases
may be made at the beginning and/or end of a
row, or at set places within the row. You also can
narrow your work by skipping one or more
stitches, but this method can leave holes. Unless
you want the decorative effect created by holes,
it is preferable to decrease by the method
shown here (see right) or by crocheting two or
more stitches together, in a stitch cluster (see
page 23).

When working single decrease clusters one
above another, in mid row, work consistently
either the first or second part of the cluster into
the top of the previous cluster to maintain the
lines of decrease.

*Decreasing plays an important role in shaping a
garment to fit (see page 40).*

MULTIPLE DECREASES

You can decrease by more than one stitch at the ends of rows by omitting stitches.
At the beginning of rows, you slip stitch over the number of stitches you want to
decrease and at the ends you simply leave stitches unworked. This method creates
a sharp angle. To create a more gradual decrease, work stitches together in a
cluster (see page 23). Double crochet (dc) is shown here, but the method is the
same for all basic stitches. The turning chain counts as a stitch.

AT THE BEGINNING OF A ROW

*Work slip st (sl st) over each stitch (st) to
be subtracted. Then make the required
turning chain (t-ch) to form a new edge
st. Continue the row in pattern.*

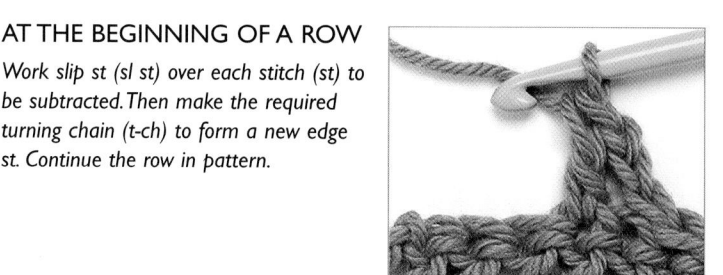

AT THE END OF A ROW

*Work in pattern until you reach the sts
to be decreased. Leave these sts
unworked, turn and make the t-ch for the
first stitch of the next row.*

WORKING A STITCH CLUSTER

To decrease one, two, three, etc. stitches, work two, three, four, etc. stitches together. At the beginning of a row, when the turning chain counts as the first stitch, work the second and third stitches together to make a single decrease and the second, third, and fourth together to make a double decrease. At the end of a row, work the last two, three, or four stitches together. In mid row, work one, two, or three consecutive stitches together in the appropriate positions. The steps here describe single and double decreases at the beginning of rows for single, half double, and double crochet. The method is the same for longer crochet stitches, such as triple crochet.

SINGLE CROCHET (sc)

Single decrease: Chain (ch) 1 (counts as 1 sc), skip first stitch (st), *insert hook into 2nd st, wrap the yarn round the hook (yo) and it draw through**; rep from *once more into 3rd st (3 loops on hook), ending yo and draw through all loops—single decrease (sc2tog) made.

Double decrease: Work as for single decrease from *, but rep from * to ** once more into 4th st (4 loops on hook) before ending. Double decrease (sc3tog) made.

HALF DOUBLE CROCHET (hdc)

Single decrease: Ch 2 (counts as 1 hdc), skip first st, *yo, insert hook into 2nd st, yo and draw through**; rep from * once more into 3rd st (5 loops on hook), ending yo and draw through all loops—single decrease (hdc2tog) made.

Double decrease: Work as for single decrease from *, but rep from * to ** once more into 4th st (7 loops on hook) before ending. Double decrease (hdc3tog) made.

DOUBLE CROCHET (dc)

Single decrease: Ch 3 (counts as 1 dc), skip first st, *yo, insert hook into 2nd st, yo and draw through, yo and draw through 2 loops only**; rep from * once more into 3rd st (3 loops on hook), ending yo and draw through all loops—single decrease (dc2tog) made.

Double decrease: Work as for single decrease from *, but rep from * to ** once more into 4th st (4 loops on hook) before ending. Double decrease (dc3tog) made.

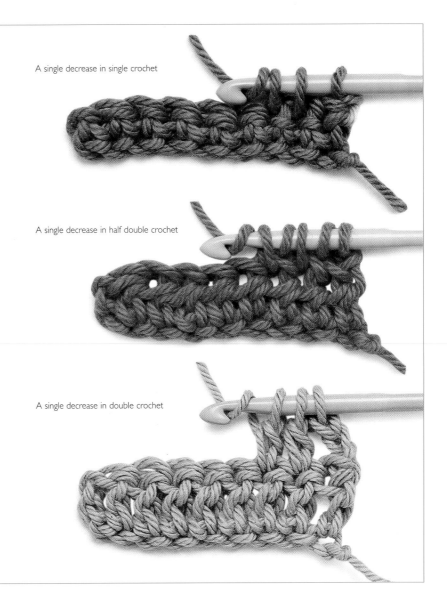

A single decrease in single crochet

A single decrease in half double crochet

A single decrease in double crochet

FOLLOWING PATTERNS

Crochet pattern instructions indicate, in abbreviated form, how many and what kind of stitches to work and where to insert the hook. They assume you are familiar with the basic stitches and other procedures and that you understand these abbreviations.

UNLESS OTHERWISE SPECIFIED:

- *Do not turn the work at the end of a row/round.*
- *Always count the turning chain as a stitch (see page 17).*
- *Work into the next available stitch in the previous row.*
- *Always insert the hook under both top loops of a stitch, unless it is a chain space or loop.*
- *The instruction, 1 sc, means work one single crochet into next sitch, and 5 dc means work 1 dc into each of next 5 sts.*
- *For a cluster, the instruction dc3tog or tr5tog, means that each stitch is worked into a separate stitch, before joining.*
- *If all parts of the cluster are to be worked into the next stitch, the instruction would say dc5tog in next.*
- *The instruction to work "even" in a pattern means to work without any increasing or decreasing.*

MULTIPLES

In the stitch glossaries the pattern gives the number of stitches required in the row and the number of chains to work for the foundation chain in this way: Multiple of 5 sts plus 2, plus 2 for foundation ch. This means make 9, 14, 19, etc, chains in order to work with 7, 12, 17, etc. stitches.

BRACKETS [ ] OR PARENTHESES ( )

These are used in three distinct ways:
- *To simplify repetition—see Repeats (below).*
- *To indicate at the end of a row/round the total number of stitches that have been worked in that row/round. For example, (24 dc) means that the row/round counts as 24 double crochet stitches.*
- *To give information about different sizes.*

RIGHT SIDE/WRONG SIDE (rs/ws)

Even if a crochet pattern is reversible it is usual to define a right side. When working in the round, the right side is normally facing you. Where the work is turned between rows, instructions specify the first right side row. If you are directed to keep the right side facing you when working rows, bind off at the end of each row and rejoin the yarn.

REPEATS

*Instructions in brackets are worked the number of times stated, ie: [ch 1, skip 1 ch, 1 dc] 5 times. A single asterisk marks the beginning of a pattern repeat sequence. For example *ch 1, skip 1 ch, 1 dc; rep from * across. A double asterisk indicates a smaller repeat in the main repeat sequence. The instruction: rep from * to last st means work complete repeats until one stitch remains.*

across	to the end of the row
alt	alternate
approx	approximate(ly)
beg	beginning
bet	between
bl	insert hook under back loop only. Example: blsc—back loop single crochet
ch(s)	chain or chain stitch(es)
ch sp(s)	chain space(s)
cl	cluster
cont	continue
dc	double crochet
dc2tog	work 2 dc together
dec	decrease
dtr	double triple crochet
dtr2tog	work 2 dtr together
fl	insert hook under front loop only. Example: flsc—front loop single crochet
foll	following
gr	group
hdc	half double crochet
hdc2tog	work 2 hdc together
in next	sts to be worked into same stitch
inc	increase
lp(s)	loop(s)
nc	not closed (see Clusters, page 73)

patt	pattern
p or pc	picot
rf	raised front. Example: rfsc—raised front single crochet
rb	raised back. Example: rbsc—raised back single crochet
rem	remaining
rep	repeat
rnd	round
sc	single crochet
sc2tog	work 2 sc together
sk	skip
sl st	slip stitch
sp(s)	space(s)
st(s)	stitch(es)
t-ch(s)	turning chain(s)
tog	together
tr	triple or treble crochet
tr2tog	work 2 tr together
yo	yarn over hook
*	Work instructions immediately following *, then repeat as directed, (see Repeats, page 24)
[ ]	Work or repeat all instructions enclosed in brackets as directed immediately after, (see Repeats, page 24)

FINISHING AND JOINING

For a polished, professional look, take special care when finishing and joining your work—its whole appearance and durability depend on it. Make sure all stray ends of yarn are woven neatly and securely into the wrong side. Seams can be sewn or joined with a crochet hook.

BLOCKING AND PRESSING

Cotton lace work usually needs careful pinning and pressing. Other crochet, particularly a textured piece, hardly ever requires this treatment. Pinning the article, misting with a fine spray, and leaving it to dry naturally may be just as effective. Afghan stitch pieces may need more blocking (see page 82). Be sure to use rust-proof pins.

To join pieces of crochet work, it is often simplest to stitch them together, using matching yarn and a tapestry needle. But you can also use crochet stitches to join seams. These seams are strong and quick to work. Using slip stitch to join two pieces together gives the most invisible seam. Single crochet will form a ridge at the seam that can be a feature on the right side. The number of stitches to work per row end is the same as for edgings (see page 86).

When you are joining motifs, those with straight edges can be joined in the normal way. However, when there are many pieces, particularly squares and triangles, it is worthwhile connecting pairs of motifs in a continuous seam to avoid repeated fastening off (see page 27).

Piecing together different patches of crocheted motifs is a classic way to assemble a garment—as in this granny square top (see page 64–65).

SLIP-STITCH SEAM

Place the pieces right sides together. *Insert hook through both edge stitches, wrap the yarn round the hook (yo) and draw through to complete 1 slip stitch (sl st); rep from *, working loosely.

FLAT SLIP-STITCH SEAM

Place the pieces edge to edge and wrong sides up. Work 1 sl st into each edge alternately. (See also alternative, below.)

SINGLE-CROCHET SEAM

Place the pieces right sides together (or wrong sides together for a visible seam) and work as for slip-stitch seam, using single crochet (sc) instead of sl st.

SINGLE-CROCHET AND CHAIN SEAM

A useful variation on single-crochet seam, this is used when less bulk and/or greater flexibility is needed. Work 1 sc and 1 chain (ch) alternately.

ALTERNATIVE FLAT SLIP STITCH

A neat, flat seam may be made using the tops of stitches, as for example, with motifs made in the round. Lay the pieces edge to edge and right sides up. Insert the hook down through the top loop only of each corresponding pair of stitches and join with slip stitch.

Many motifs have a final round of picots or loops, and these may be used to join motifs to each other as that round is being worked. Typically the center chain of a loop is replaced by a sl st or sc worked into a loop of the adjacent motif.

After joining, small motifs, which add decoration and strength, can be worked in the spaces between. The main motifs shown here are Flower Wheel, (see page 54). For the filler motifs, work a foundation ring of 5 ch (see page 53), then in round 1 [1 sc in ring, ch 2, sl st in motif, ch 2, 1 sc in ring] 4 times.

SIMPLE SASH BELT

Practice your basic crochet skills by making this simple belt to wear with jeans, a dress—virtually anything. You can dress it up with a fantastic selection of beads and trimmings.

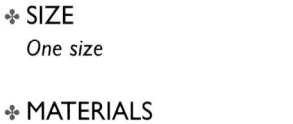

❖ SIZE
One size

❖ MATERIALS
Yarn Tweed-effect knitting worsted,
1 x 50 g ball
Hooks One size H crochet hook
Notions Needle and thread,
beads and other trimmings

❖ GAUGE
10 sts and 10 rows = 2½" (6 cm)

❖ SKILLS USED
Chain (ch), p11; double crochet
(dc), p15

See page 24–25 for pattern
abbreviations.

STRING BIKINI TOP

This bikini top uses only single crochet, chain stitch, and slip stitch. The straps are made with a long string of chain stitches with single crochets added to each one for more strength. Pair it with shorts, jeans, or a sarong. Gently shaped, it will mold itself to your contours.

❖ SIZE
One size: To fit 34–36"
(86–91 cm) bust

❖ MATERIALS
Yarn Cotton glacé 100% cotton,
2 x 50 g balls
Hooks One size D crochet hook

❖ GAUGE
24 sts and 21 rows = 4"
(10 cm)

❖ SKILLS USED
Chain (ch), p11; slip stitch (sl st),
p11; single crochet (sc), p13;
rejoining yarn, p39

See page 24–25 for pattern
abbreviations.

SIMPLE SASH BELT

Using knitting worsted and size H hook, ch 10; turn. Work in rows of dc until you have used up the whole ball of yarn. Fasten off.

FINISHING

Using needle and thread, stitch beads and patch motifs to the ends of the belt.

BEADED DETAILS

Stitching beads to the ends of this belt gives it extra visual interest and detail as well as adding some useful weight that will make the ends hang nicely when the belt is tied.

This belt has been made in a tweed-effect yarn that is mainly turquoise in color, with little flecks of other colors. These shades are picked up in the beads that have been used. Fabric flowers motifs in the same colorway have been stitched along the ends.

Match your beads to your chosen yarn, they come in all shades, shapes and sizes, so you're bound to find something to suit.

BIKINI TOP
LEFT CUP

Using cotton glacé and size D hook, ch 36; turn.

Row 1: Ch 2, 1 sc in each ch to end; turn. Repeat this row 14 more times.

Row 16: Ch 2, 17 sc; turn. Repeat row 16, 14 more times.

You will now have an L-shaped piece, measuring 6" (15 cm) on the longer edges and 3" (7.5 cm) on the shorter edges. Stitch the two short edges of the 'L' together, starting at the point where they meet at a right angle.

RIGHT CUP

Make this in the same way. Opposite side will be the right side.

FINISHING

Take the left cup: Starting at beginning of original foundation ch (this is inner edge), join yarn: Ch 2, sc to end; work 90 ch, (this is the neck strap); turn. Ch 2, 89 sc back along the ch. Then work 36 sc, evenly spaced, along the outer edge, to the outer corner; work 90 ch (this is the back strap); turn. Ch 2, 89 sc back along the ch. Then work 36 sc, evenly spaced, along the lower edge, until you reach the inner corner. Work 4 ch (to make the strap that joins the two cups), then join with a sl st to inner corner of right cup. Then work along the inner edge; work 90 ch (neck strap); turn. Ch 2, 89 sc, back along the ch. Then

CHANGING THE SIZE

To make the bra top slightly larger, simply work an extra row of sc all round after making up. An extra row of sc will also make the straps slightly wider.

work 36 sc, evenly spaced, along the outer edge, to the outer corner; work 90 ch (back strap); turn. Ch 2, 89 sc back along the ch. Then work 36 sc, evenly spaced, along the lower edge, until you reach the inner corner. Work 4 sc along the joining strap. Break yarn and fasten off.

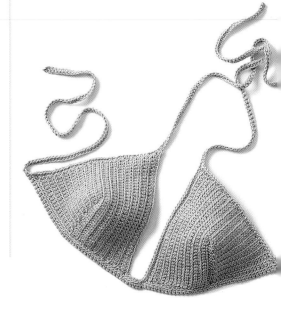

BASIC STITCH VARIATIONS

You can achieve interesting textural effects by adapting the basic stitches. Inserting the hook into a different part of the work instead of into the top two loops of each stitch will change the look of a basic crochet stitch.

You can insert your hook in a variety of different ways. For example, you can work under one top loop at a time, between the stitches, or around the post or stem of the stitch. All crochet stitches can be worked with these variations, but some produce more interesting effects than others. As well as adding surface texture, these stitches will make a garment thicker and warmer. To begin any of these stitch variations, first make a foundation chain and work one row in your chosen stitch.

Stitch worked into back loop

Stitch worked into front loop

Simply working between two stitches can make an interesting texture, as seen in this pillow cover (see page 36).

WORKING UNDER ONE LOOP

By continually working into only the back loop (abbreviated as *bl*, as in *blsc*), you can create a pattern with a ridged effect. Working into only the front loop (*fl*) makes a less pronounced ridge with a horizontal line. This technique works well with the shorter stitches, for example single crochet and double crochet.

TO WORK INTO THE BACK LOOP

From the 2nd row onward work your chosen crochet stitch normally (for example, half double crochet as shown here), but insert the hook into the back loop of each stitch.

TO WORK INTO THE FRONT LOOP

From the 2nd row onward work your chosen crochet stitch normally (for example, single crochet as shown here), but insert the hook into the front loop only of each stitch.

WORKING BETWEEN TWO STITCHES

This technique of working between the stitches of the previous row is quick and easy, and produces a slightly thicker fabric with a more open look.

TO WORK BETWEEN TWO STITCHES

From the 2nd row onward work your chosen crochet stitch normally (for example, double crochet as shown here), but insert the hook between posts and below all horizontal yarns connecting stitches.

WORKING SPIKES

Spikes are arrow-shaped loops of yarn on the surface of the work. They are made by inserting the hook lower down than usual, for example, into one or more rows below the previous one (pattern instructions will always specify where).

TO MAKE A SIMPLE SINGLE CROCHET SPIKE

Insert the hook into the base of the next stitch, wrap the yarn round the hook (yo) and draw it through up to the height of a single crochet (sc) in this row, (2 loops on hook) (right). Yo and draw it through both loops. Single crochet (sc) spike made.

MORE BASIC VARIATIONS

RAISED STITCHES

A raised effect can be achieved by working around the posts of the stitches in the previous row, either in the front (raised front, abbreviated rf), or in the back (raised back, abbreviated rb). Rows can be worked all in front or all in back, or alternatively one or more stitches around the back then one or more stitches around the front, to produce a large variety of different stitch patterns.

LINKED STITCHES

Longer stitches can be linked to each other down their sides to eliminate the space between the stems of the stitches. This creates an effect as if several rows of shorter stitches had been worked in the same direction at the same time.

Surprisingly easy variations on the basic stitches can create some very different looks in crochet (see page 50).

WORKING RAISED STITCHES

To make raised stitches you don't work into the top loops of the previous row, instead, you work into the posts of the stitches in the previous row. The posts are the vertical chains formed by the crochet, more obvious in the longer stitches.

TO WORK RAISED STITCHES AROUND THE FRONT

First work a row of your basic stitch, such as the double crochet (dc) shown here. From the 2nd row onward, make each stitch normally, but insert the hook from right to left under the post of the stitch below (left), on the front of the work. Wrap the yarn round the hook (yo) and pull through the post, then continue as you would for the chosen stitch (right).

TO WORK RAISED STITCHES AROUND THE BACK

Work exactly the same as for raised stitches to the front, but insert the hook on the back of the work, from right to left around the post of the stitch below (left). Yo and pull through the post, then continue as you would for the chosen stitch (right).

WORKING LINKED STITCHES

1 *Insert the hook down through the upper of the 2 horizontal loops around the post of the last stitch made (shown here in triple stitch); wrap the yarn around the hook (yo).*

2 *Draw a loop through, insert the hook down through the lower horizontal loop of the same stitch, yo and draw a loop through. (There are now 3 loops on hook.)*

3 *Insert the hook for the next stitch, yo, draw it through the stitch only, [yo and draw it through 2 loops only] 3 times. Linked triple is made. Continue to the end of the row; turn.*

4 *To start a row with a linked triple, treat the 2nd and 4th chains from the hook as the upper and lower horizontal loops of the last stitch made.*

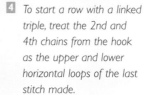

BACK AND FRONT LOOP HALF DOUBLE CROCHET

Multiple of 2 sts, plus 1 for foundation ch.

Row 1: Skip 2 ch, hdc across, turn.
Row 2: Ch 2, *1 blhdc, 1 flhdc; rep from * to last st, 1 hdc, turn.
Row 2 forms the pattern.

BACK LOOP HALF DOUBLE CROCHET

Any number of sts, plus 1 for foundation ch.

Row 1: Skip 2 ch, hdc across, turn.
Row 2: Ch 2, blhdc across, turn.
Row 2 forms the pattern.

BACK AND FRONT LOOP SINGLE CROCHET

Multiple of 2 sts, plus 1 for foundation ch.

Row 1: Skip 2 ch, sc across, turn.
Row 2: Ch 1, *1 blsc, 1 flsc; rep from * to last st, 1 sc, turn.
Row 2 forms the pattern.

ALTERNATE ROWS BACK AND FRONT LOOP DOUBLE CROCHET

Any number of sts, plus 2 for foundation ch.

Row 1: Skip 3 ch, dc across, turn.
Row 2: Ch 3, bldc across, turn.
Row 3: Ch 3, fldc across, turn.
Rows 2 and 3 form the pattern.

HALF DOUBLE CROCHET BETWEEN STITCHES

Any number of sts, plus 1 for foundation ch.

Row 1: Skip 2 ch, hdc across, turn.
Row 2: Ch 2, *1 hdc inserting hook between posts of next 2 sts and below all horizontal connecting threads; rep from * across, turn.
Row 2 forms the pattern.

1 x 1 RAISED DOUBLE CROCHET RIB

Multiple of 2 sts, plus 2 for foundation ch.

Row 1 (wrong side): Skip 3 ch, dc across, turn.

Row 2: Ch 2, *1 rfdc, 1 rbdc; rep from * to last st, 1 rfdc, turn.

Row 2 forms the pattern.

DOUBLE CROCHET BETWEEN STITCHES

Any number of sts, add ch 2 for foundation ch.

Row 1: Skip 3 ch, dc across, turn.

Row 2: Ch 3, *1 dc inserting hook between posts of next 2 sts and below all horizontal connecting threads; rep from * across, turn.

Row 2 forms the pattern.

DEEP RIDGED RAISED DOUBLE CROCHET

Any number of sts, plus 2 for foundation ch.

Row 1 (right side): Skip 3 ch, dc across, turn.

Row 2: Ch 2, rfdc across, turn.

Row 2 forms the pattern.

BACK LOOP SPIKED SINGLE CROCHET

Multiple of 4 sts plus 1, plus 1 for foundation ch.

Special abbreviation

sc spike (single crochet spike): Insert hook into base of st, ie. 1 more row down, then complete sc normally.

Row 1 (right side): Skip 2 ch, sc across, turn.

Row 2: Ch 1, blsc across, turn.

Row 3: Ch 1, *1 sc spike, 3 blsc; rep from * across, turn.

Row 4: As row 2.

Row 5: Ch 1, *2 blsc, 1 sc spike, 1 blsc ; rep from * across, turn.

Rows 2 to 5 form the pattern.

ALTERNATING SPIKED SINGLE CROCHET

Multiple of 2 sts plus 1, plus 1 for foundation ch.

Special abbreviation

sc spike (single crochet spike): Insert hook into base of st, ie. 1 more row down, then complete sc normally.

Row 1 (right side): Skip 2 ch, sc across, turn.

Row 2: Ch 1, 1 sc spike, *1 sc, 1 sc spike; rep from * to last st, 1 sc, turn.

Row 3: Ch 1, 1 sc, *1 sc spike, 1 sc; rep from * to last st 1 sc, turn.

Rows 2 and 3 form the pattern.

PEEK-A-BOO PILLOW COVER

This is an easy project for learning to crochet between the stitches. The stitch creates holes through which you can see the pillow. Start with a purchased pillow in a solid, bright color. Trim the corners of the pillow cover with pompoms if you like.

❖ **SIZE**
One size: 12" wide and 16" long (32 x 47 cm)

❖ **MATERIALS**
Yarn Knitting worsted 100% cotton, 4 x 50 g balls color A, 1 x 50g ball color B
Hooks One size 8 crochet hook
Notions 12 x 16" (30 x 41 cm) solid-color pillow, cardboard (to make pompoms)

❖ **GAUGE**
21 sts and 9 rows = 4" (10 cm) over pattern

❖ **SKILLS USED**
Chain (ch), p11; double crochet (dc), p15; raised stitches, p32–35; finishing and joining, p26–27

See page 24–25 for pattern abbreviations.

PEEK-A-BOO PILLOW COVER

Using color A and size 8 hook, ch 39; turn.

Row 1: Skip 3 ch, 1 dc in each ch to end; turn.

Row 2: Ch 3, *1 dc, inserting hook between posts of next 2 sts of previous row and below all horizontal connecting threads; repeat from * to end; turn.

Next and all subsequent rows: Repeat row 2 until work measures 38½" (98 cm).

HOW TO MAKE A POMPOM

Cut two circles of card 4" (10 cm) in diameter and cut a hole 1½" (4 cm) in diameter from the center of each. Place the two rings of card together and wind the yarn around and around the rings until the center holes are completely filled. Snip through the layers of yarn at the outer edge, slipping the scissor blades between the two pieces of card. Slip a 10" (25 cm) length of yarn between the two card rings and tie firmly around the center of the bunch of yarn. Slip off the card and you will have a pompom. Trim with scissors to neaten but leave the length of yarn long.

FINISHING

Lay the work flat and press lightly. Fold over 8" (20 cm) at one end and 14½" (36 cm) at the other end. The two short edges should overlap. Stitch the two long edges of the pillow together. Alternatively, work a row of sc along the long edges, through both layers, to make a decorative crocheted edge.

Divide the color B yarn into four equal lengths and use to make four pompoms (see box below). When finishing the pompoms, leave long ends of yarn and use these to thread through the holes in the stitches at each corner of the pillow and knot the pompoms firmly in place. Insert the pillow into the lapped opening.

CHANGING COLORS

Different colored yarns are used to create stripes, geometric patterns, and simple pictures in sharp contrasts or subtle gradations. Crochet stitches are generally larger and more varied than knitted ones and are perfect for overlapped and relief effects as well as multicolored rows.

TEXTURED EFFECTS

Richly textured effects can be achieved using different types of yarn along with changes of color. Multicolored yarns create a new effect when combined with plain colors or textured yarns. Bouclé and mohair multicolored yarns are shown worked together in this basketweave pattern sample.

When working with color, you can use a single yarn, or strands of more than one to give both variegated color and additional warmth. Yarns may be plain color, two-tone, or patterned in different ways—heather mixtures, mottled, or multicolored yarns.

Use single colors for one or more whole rows to create horizontal stripes. Carry the yarns not in use up the side of the work or cut them off and rejoin as required.

For blocks of color, such as vertical stripes or intarsia, join a separate ball for each area or stripe, to avoid floats entirely. There is no need (as there is in knitting) to twist the yarns around each other at the point where they change over to prevent holes appearing.

When yarn is joined at the middle of a row, the yarn not in use is carried along the back of the work. This will form loops, or floats, which may catch during wear; these must be worked over every few stitches, or encased during right side rows.

CHARTS

Most multicolor patterns are shown as graphs, in which each square corresponds to one stitch—normally single crochet, since it is the smallest, squarest stitch. There are two main rules for following color chart grids: always change to the next color required just before you complete the previous stitch, and follow odd-numbered rows from right to left and even-numbered from left to right (a chart always represents the right side of the work).

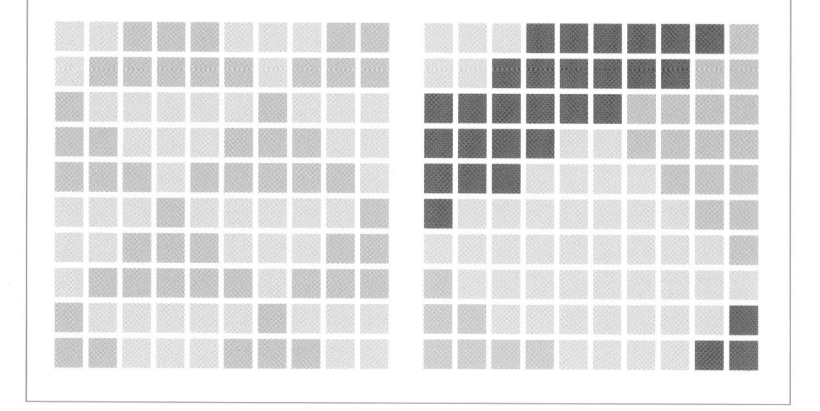

YARN ENDS

Provided you can do so without interfering with the visual effect, work over yarn ends whenever possible. Remember that all stray ends must finally be woven into the wrong side.

JOINING NEW YARN

When working horizontal stripes, change to the new yarn at the end of the row just before completing the last stitch. This way, the new color is ready to work the turning chain. When working in the round, work the last stitch with the old color and use the new color to make the joining slip stitch.

1 *Before you pick up for the last time to make the last stitch with the old color, drop the old yarn and pick up the new.*

2 *Draw new yarn through to complete the old stitch—the working loop is now in the new color. Before working the next stitch, make sure old yarn is kept to the wrong side of the work, or carried along the tops of the next few stitches so that it will become encased.*

CHANGING YARN

Change the yarns as for joining, just before you complete the last stitch with the old color. Draw up the float in the new color evenly, making sure the old yarn is appropriately positioned. Single crochet is illustrated here, but the same principle applies to all other basic stitches.

REJOINING YARN

Occasionally you will need to join yarn into a piece of crochet that has been fastened off, in order to make a fresh start.

1 *Insert the hook into the appropriate place. Start with a slip knot (or a simple loop, if you prefer) and draw this through.*

2 *Make the appropriate turning chain for the first new stitch (chain 3 for 1 double crochet is shown here).*

FLOATS

To help the tension of floats be more even, catch them into the work every few stitches. When finished, cut in half any unacceptably long float yarns and weave them in.

STRIPED HALTER TOP

Great when you want to sparkle and shine at a party, this top is dazzlingly different, easy to make, and takes only five balls of yarn.

❖ SIZE
*One size: To fit 34–36" (86–91 cm) bust. Finished size
22" (56 cm) at widest point*

❖ MATERIALS
*Yarn Sport weight lurex yarn, 3 x 50 g balls color A,
2 x 50 g balls color B
Hook One size 3 crochet hook*

❖ GAUGE
25 sts and 23 rows = 4" (10 cm)

❖ SKILLS USED
*Chain (ch), p11; single crochet (sc), p13; increasing,
p20–21; decreasing, p22–23; changing color and rejoining
yarn, p39*

See page 24–25 for pattern abbreviations.

STRIPED HALTER TOP

Using color A and size 3 hook, ch 4; 2 sc in 3rd ch from hook; turn (3 sts).

Work in rows of sc, increasing 1 st at each end of every row, until you have 9 sts. Then join in color B and work 2 rows, increasing 1 st at either end of both rows. Continue like this, working in stripes of 2 rows of alternate colors and increasing 1 st at the beginning and end of every row, until you have 139 sts.

Work 14 rows without shaping.

To make the bra top, work 68 sts and turn. Work in rows of sc, maintaining the striped pattern, decreasing 1 st at each end of every row, until you have 6 sts. Continue on these stitches, in main color and without further shaping, for 96 rows, to make halter strap. Break off yarn, rejoin and work second side of bra top in the same way; break off yarn.

BORDER AND STRAPS

Join yarn to point at base of garment. Work 2 turning ch and 2 sc in same st, then 69 sc, evenly spaced, up left-hand

YARN INFORMATION

This kind of yarn is quick to work with but has a tendency to twist. To prevent tangles, keep a rubber band around the ball of yarn and let out a little yarn at a time—about 12" (30 cm).

side. Ch 84 (this is the back tie); turn. Ch 2 then work 83 sc back to start of ch. Work 19 sc up back edge. Then ch 84 (this is the second back tie); turn. Ch 2 then work 83 sc back to start of ch. Work 31 sc up left outer side of bra top. Work 95 sc along edge of halter strap and 3 sc in corner st; 5 sc along end of strap; 3 sc in corner st; 95 sc down other edge of strap. Work 31 sc down inner side of bra top, 1 sc in center stitch, 31 sc up inner side of right bra top; continue border around second halter strap in exactly the same way as the first, sc 31 down right outer side. Make a third back tie in same way as first and second; work19 sc down right back edge. Make a fourth tie, as before; work 70 sc down right-hand side; join with a sl st at 2nd ch of t-ch. Fasten off yarn.

FANCY STITCHES

One of the great strengths of crochet is the versatility of the stitches.

Change the height of your stitches from row to row, and you

will see many different textures and stripe widths.

As you are working a row of crochet, making stitches of different heights will produce wave shapes and surface texture. Additional texture can be achieved by crossing stitches to produce a cable effect, or working them into different

places. Making long stitches—reaching down below the level of the previous row and picking up around the post—will result in raised surface stitches, which look particularly striking when worked in contrasting colors.

RAISED SURFACE STITCHES

There are many variations of raised surface stitches, but they are all made in a similar way. The method shown below involves skipping stitches in the background fabric and working around the post. The surface stitches must be longer than the background stitches. When skipping a stitch would result in a hole, work the raised surface stitch together with the background stitch, like a decrease cluster (see page 23). In this typical example the background is made with alternate rows of single crochet (sc) and double crochet (dc).

Skip stitches (sts) in sc row and work raised surface sts in dc around the post of the chosen stitch. Work at the front, alternately a few sts to left and then to right, inserting hook from right to left.

Leaving the last loop of each stitch (st) on the hook, work raised surface st, then background sc (there are now 3 loops on hook). Wrap yarn round hook (yo) and draw through all loops to complete the cluster.

SIMPLE CROSSED STITCH

1. To make a pair of simple crossed stitches (double crochet shown here), first skip 1 st and work 1 dc into next stitch. Wrap the yarn round hook (yo) and insert the hook into the previous skipped stitch.

2. Pick the yarn up and draw through, then yo to work 1 dc.

3. The crossed dc wraps up and encases the previous dc.

CABLE CROSSED STITCH (back)

1. To begin cable crossed stitch, first skip 3 sts and then work 3 double triple (dtr) normally (shown here worked on dc).

2. With hook behind sts, insert it from front. Work 1 dtr into each of 3 skipped sts.

CABLE CROSSED STITCH (front)

Work entirely in the front of the previous stitches (holding them aside at the back if necessary) after inserting the hook, so as not to encase the stitches, as in Simple Crossed Stitch (left).

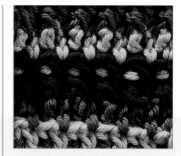

SINGLE CROCHET AND SPIKE CLUSTERS

Multiple of 8 sts plus 5, plus 1 for foundation ch.

Special abbreviation spcl (spike cluster): Over next st pick up 5 spike loops by inserting hook as follows: 2 sts to right and 1 row down; 1 st to right and 2 rows down; directly over next st and 3 rows down; 1st to left and 2 rows down; 2 sts to left and 1 row down, (6 loops on hook); insert hook into top of next st in current row itself, yo, draw loop through, yo drawn through all 7 loops on hook.

Work 4 rows each in colors A, B, and C throughout.

Note: T-ch does not count as a stitch.

Row 1 (right side): Skip 1 ch, sc across, turn.

Row 2: Ch 1, sc across, turn.

Rows 3 and 4: As row 2.

Row 5: Ch 1, 4 sc, *1 spcl, 7 sc; rep from * to last st, 1 sc, turn.

Rows 6 to 8: As row 2.

Rows 5 to 8 form the pattern.

INTERLOCKING DOUBLE CROCHET SHELLS

Multiple of 6 sts plus 1, plus 1 for foundation ch.

Work 1 row each in colors A, B, and C.

Row 1 (right side): Skip 1 ch, 1 sc, *skip 2 ch, 5 dc in next—called shell, skip 2 ch, 1 sc; rep from * across, turn.

Row 2: Ch 3, 2 dc in first st, *1 sc in 3rd dc of shell, 1 shell in sc; rep from * to last shell, 1 sc in 3rd dc of shell, 3 dc in sc, turn.

Row 3: Ch 1, *1 shell in sc, 1 sc in 3rd dc of shell; rep from * across with last sc in t-ch, turn.

Rows 2 and 3 form the pattern.

ALTERNATING RELIEF STITCH

Multiple of 2 sts plus 1, plus 2 for foundation ch.

Work 1 row each in colors A, B, and C.

Row 1 (right side): Skip 3 ch, dc across, turn.

Row 2: Ch 3, *1 rftr, 1 dc; rep from * across, turn.

Row 2 forms the pattern.

INSET FLOWER BUDS

Multiple of 10 sts plus 3, plus 2 for foundation ch.

Worked with color A and with B and C for the flower buds.

Row 1 (right side): With A, skip 3 ch, 2 dc, *ch 3, skip 3 ch, 1 sc, ch 3, skip 3 ch, 3 dc; rep from * across, turn.

Row 2: Ch 2, 2rbdc, *ch 3, skip 3 ch, 1 sc in sc, ch 3, skip 3 ch, 3 rbdc; rep from * across, turn.

Row 3: Ch 2, 2 rfdc, *ch 1, skip 3 ch, 5 dc in sc, ch 1, skip 3 ch, 3 rfdc; rep from * across. Do not turn but work flower buds in B and C alternately over each group of 5 dc thus: Ch 3, dc4tog, ch 1. Bind off—flowerbud completed. Turn.

Row 4: With A, ch 3, 2 rbtr, *ch 3, 1 sc in ch at top of flowerbud, ch 3, skip 1 ch, 3 rbtr; rep from * across, turn.

Row 5. As row 2.

Rows 2 to 5 form the pattern.

CHECKERED DOUBLE CROCHET

Multiple of 4 sts plus 2, plus 2 for foundation ch.

Work 1 row each in colors A, B, and C.

Row 1 (right side): Skip 3 ch, 1 dc, *ch 2, skip 2 ch, 2 dc; rep from * across, turn.

Row 2: No t-ch, working into foundation ch over ch sps of row 1 *ch 2, skip 2 dc, 2 dc; rep from * to last 2 sts, ch 1, skip 1, 1 sl st, turn.

Row 3: Ch 3, working into last-but-one row over ch sps of last row, 1 dc, *ch 2, skip 2 dc, 2 dc; rep from * across, turn.

Row 4: Working into last-but-one row over ch sps of last row *ch 2, skip 2 dc, 2 dc ; rep from * to last 2 sts, ch 1, skip 1, 1 sl st, turn.

Rows 3 and 4 form the pattern.

SINGLE AND DOUBLE CROCHET STRIPES

Any number of sts, plus 1 for foundation ch.

Work 2 rows each in colors A and B alternately, or 1 row each in A, B, and C.

Row 1 (right side): Skip 2 ch, sc across, turn.

Row 2: Ch 1, sc across, turn.

Row 3: Ch 3, dc across, turn.

Row 4: As row 3.

Row 5, 6, 7 and 8: As row 2.

Rows 3 to 8 form the pattern.

MULTISTITCH WAVE

Multiple of 14 sts plus 1, plus 1 for foundation ch.

Special abbreviations wave (worked over 14 sts): 1 sc, 2 hdc, 2 dc, 3 tr, 2 dc, 2 hdc, 2 sc. reverse wave (worked over 14 sts): 1 tr, 2 dc, 2 hdc, 3 sc, 2 hdc, 2 dc, 2 tr.

Work 2 rows each in colors A and B alternately throughout.

Row 1 (right side): Skip 2 ch, *wave; rep from * across, turn.

Row 2: Ch 1, sc across, turn.

Row 3: Ch 4, *reverse wave; rep from * across, turn.

Row 4: As row 2.

Row 5: Ch 1, *wave; rep from * across, turn.

Row 6: As row 2.

Rows 3 to 6 form the pattern.

DOUBLE CROCHET BLOCKS AND SHELLS

Multiple of 10 sts plus 7, plus 2 for foundation ch.

Worked in colors A, B, and C.

Row 1 (right side): With A, skip 3 ch, 5 dc, *with B, skip 2 ch, (2 dc, ch 2, 2 dc—called shell) in next, skip 2 ch, with A, 5 dc—called block; rep from * to last ch, 1 dc, cut B, turn.

Row 2: With A, ch 3, 5 dc over block, *with C, 1 shell over shell as follows: Skip 2 dc, 1 shell in 2 ch sp, skip 2 dc, with A, 5 dc over block; rep from * to last st, 1 dc, cut C, turn.

Row 3: With A, ch 3, with B, 1 shell in 3rd of 5 dc block, *with A, work 5 dc block over shell as follows: 2 dc, 1 dc in 2 ch sp, 2 dc, with B, 1 shell in 3rd of 5 dc block; rep from * to last st, with A, 1 dc, cut B, turn.

Row 4: With A, ch 3, with C, 1 shell over shell, *with A, 5 dc over block, with C, 1 shell over shell; rep from * to last st, with A, 1 dc, cut C, turn.

Row 5: With A, ch 3, 5 dc block over shell, *with B, 1 shell in 3rd of 5 dc block, with A, 5 dc block over shell; rep from * to last st, 1 dc, cut B, turn.

Rows 2 to 5 form the pattern.

CHEVRONS AND MOTIFS

The basic stitches can be combined with increasing and decreasing to create zigzags, chevrons, and curves. The same plain stitch, increased and decreased alternately at frequent intervals at the same place in each row, will create a zigzag shape.

If you want to change the shapes of rows as you work, for instance so that zigzags alternate with straight rows or angles reverse, then you must use stitches of graduated heights at the same time as increasing and decreasing.

By simply using increasing and decreasing in several different ways, you can achieve a variety of different effects. You can create curves and zigzags within a piece of crochet and combine these with other stitches to get interesting shapes and textures. You can also use increasing and decreasing to shape motifs—making individual pieces that you can join together to create a rich patchwork.

Zigzags and straight rows are combined in the swatch above left. Make a diamond by crocheting an increase triangle followed by a decrease triangle (left).

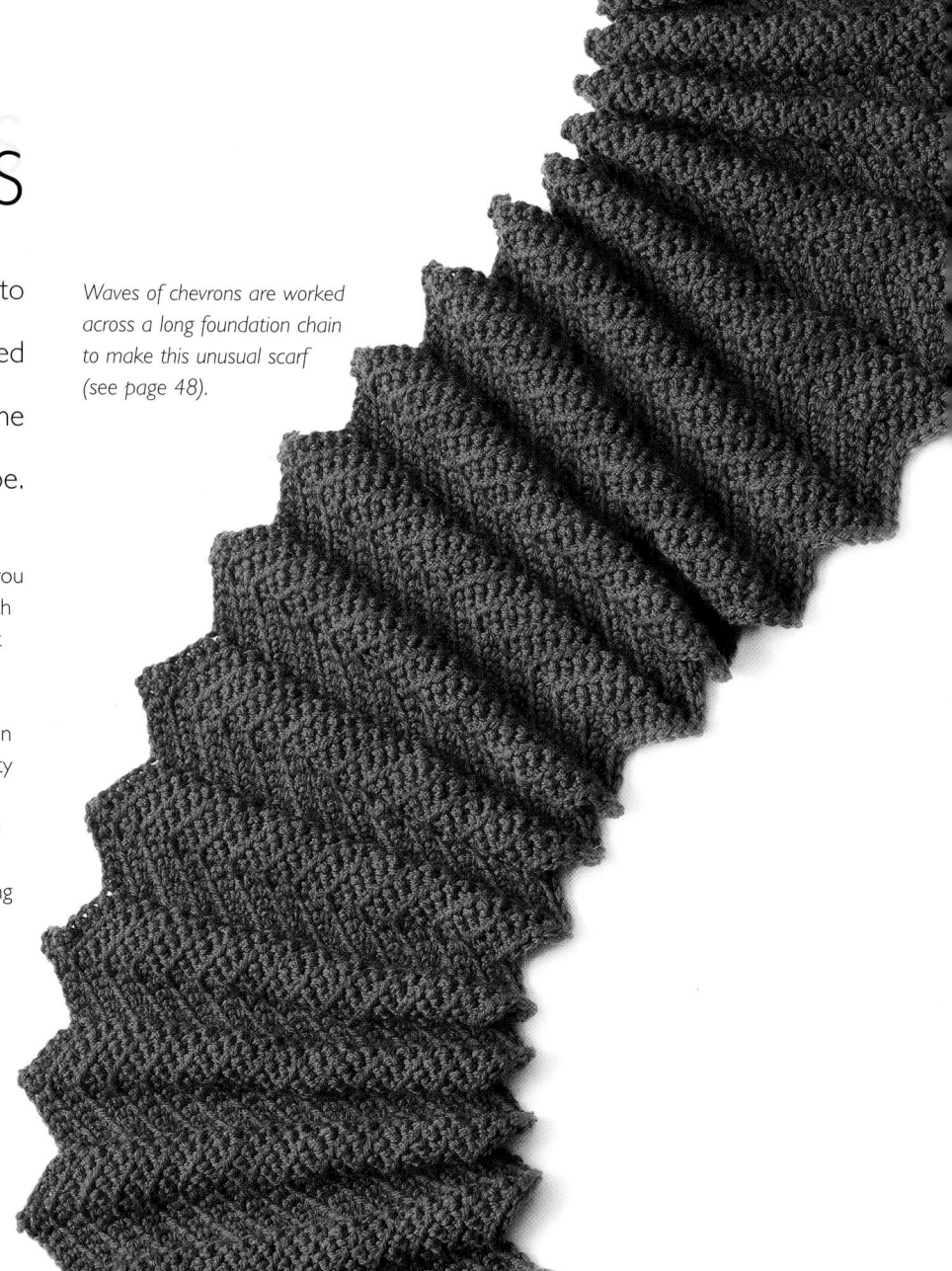

Waves of chevrons are worked across a long foundation chain to make this unusual scarf (see page 48).

SIMPLE CHEVRONS

In these patterns the same row shape is maintained and all rows are parallel throughout. If you are given the instruction to *work even* when working chevrons, you must continue increasing and decreasing as already established to create the chevrons, but keeping the same number of stitches in each row and the edges straight.

1 *Increase by working additional stitches into the same place.*

2 *Decrease by joining stitches together into clusters (see page 23).*

TRIANGLE MOTIFS

There are numerous ways of combining simple triangles (right) to make patchwork covers or bedspreads. These kind of bedcovers have long formed a large and popular part in traditional crochet.

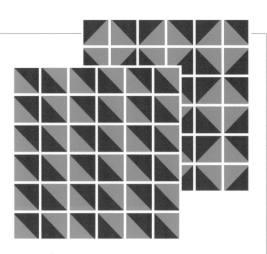

INCREASE TRIANGLE

Start with a foundation chain of 3 chains. Skip 2 ch, 2 single crochet (sc) in next, turn (3 sts—right side). Work 11 more rows in sc, making a single increase at end of every row and also at beginning of 4th, 7th, and 10th rows (17 sts at end of Row 12).

DECREASE TRIANGLE

Start with a foundation chain the desired length of a triangle side—here 18 ch. Skip 2 ch, sc across to last 2 ch, sc 2 sts together (sc2tog), turn (16 sts—right side). Work 11 rows in sc, making single decrease at end of every row and at beginning of 3rd, 6th, and 10th rows (1 st at end of row 12).

ZIGZAG SCARF

This woolly scarf has a zigzag pattern. Knit it in your own favorite color combination to coordinate with a sweater or jacket.

❖ SIZE
  One size: 10" (25 cm) wide and 45" (114 cm) long

❖ MATERIALS
  Yarn *Knitting worsted 100% wool, 2 x 50 g balls color A, 2 x 50 g balls color B*
  Hooks *One size F crochet hook*

❖ GAUGE
  8 rows = 4" (10 cm)
  1 pattern repeat = 2½" (6 cm)

❖ SKILLS USED
  Chain (ch), p11; single crochet (sc), p13; changing colors, p39; chevrons, p45

See page 24–25 for pattern abbreviations.

ZIGZAG SCARF

Using color A and size F hook, ch 283; turn.

Row 1: 1 sc into 3rd ch from hook, *5 sc, skip 3 ch, 5 sc, 3 sc into next ch, repeat from * to end but finish with 2 sc (instead of 3 sc) in last; turn.

Row 2: Ch 1, 1 sc into same st, 5 sc, skip 2 sc, 5 sc, 3 sc into next sc, rep from * to end, but finish with 2 sc.

Row 2 forms the pattern.

Repeat this row throughout, working 2 rows in alternate colors (18 rows).

WORKING IN NEW COLOR

In a piece of work like this scarf, where there are no seams, and no "right" or "wrong" side, it is important to hide yarn ends neatly or they will spoil the look of the finished piece. The color not in use should be carried up the side of the work; to avoid a loop, twist the two colored yarns together.

When you start a new ball of yarn, leave a 3 inch (7.5 cm) tail of yarn, lay this across the top of the row to be worked, and work over and around it so it becomes trapped inside the new row of stitches. When the piece is finished, break off the yarn, leaving about 3 inches (7.5 cm), and weave this neatly in and out of the stitches along the edge of the scarf. It is preferable to break the yarn, rather than cutting it, as cutting produces a blunt end which is more difficult to "hide".

CHANGING THE SIZE

To make a wider scarf, simply increase the length of the foundation chain. This chain can be any length, but should be a multiple of 14, plus 1, plus 2 for the turning chain.

To make a longer scarf, simply work more rows, until you have achieved the desired length.

If you are going to increase the size of the scarf, remember that you will need additional yarn.

TWENTY-SQUARES THROW

This cozy little blanket is made from twenty crocheted squares sewn together and given a contrasting border. The open look is achieved by working double crochet stitches into the spaces rather than into the loops.

❖ SIZE
One size: 44" (112 cm) wide and 53" (135 cm) long

❖ MATERIALS
***Yarn** Aran weight 100% merino wool, 15 x 50 g balls color A, 6 x 50 g balls color B*
***Hooks** One size 10 crochet hook*
***Notions** Tapestry needle*

❖ GAUGE
Each square measures 9" (23 cm)
11 sts and 7 rows = 4" (10 cm) over the border

❖ SKILLS USED
Chain (ch), p11; double crochet (dc), p15; joining seams, p27; changing colors and rejoining yarn, p39

See page 24–25 for pattern abbreviations.

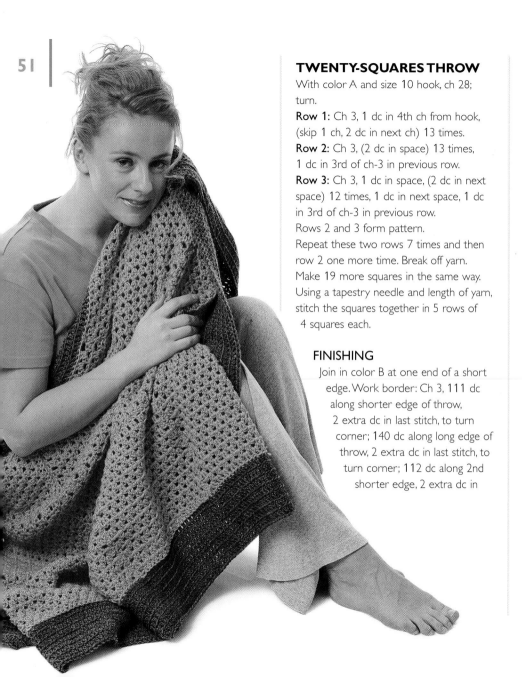

TWENTY-SQUARES THROW

With color A and size 10 hook, ch 28; turn.

Row 1: Ch 3, 1 dc in 4th ch from hook, (skip 1 ch, 2 dc in next ch) 13 times.

Row 2: Ch 3, (2 dc in space) 13 times, 1 dc in 3rd of ch-3 in previous row.

Row 3: Ch 3, 1 dc in space, (2 dc in next space) 12 times, 1 dc in next space, 1 dc in 3rd of ch-3 in previous row.

Rows 2 and 3 form pattern.

Repeat these two rows 7 times and then row 2 one more time. Break off yarn. Make 19 more squares in the same way. Using a tapestry needle and length of yarn, stitch the squares together in 5 rows of 4 squares each.

FINISHING

Join in color B at one end of a short edge. Work border: Ch 3, 111 dc along shorter edge of throw, 2 extra dc in last stitch, to turn corner; 140 dc along long edge of throw, 2 extra dc in last stitch, to turn corner; 112 dc along 2nd shorter edge, 2 extra dc in last stitch, to turn corner; 140 dc along long edge of throw, 2 extra dc in last stitch; join with sl st in 3rd of ch-3.

Work 6 more rows around border, working 3 dc into each corner st.

Note: When forming the border, you will sometimes be working along a horizontal row of the squares that make up the throw, and sometimes along an edge. When working along a horizontal row (in other words, a foundation chain edge or final row of a square), work 1 dc in each dc (28 sts along edge of square); when working along the side edge of a square, work 28 dc evenly spaced along the edge.

DIFFERENT SIZES

The throw pictured here is made up of 20 squares, each measuring 9" (23 cm) and finished with a 4" (10 cm) deep border. You could make your throw larger or smaller by making more or fewer squares and by making your border a different width.

PIECED WORK

Making a throw like this from separate squares joined together is a practical way to work. Individual squares are a manageable size and so can be worked on wherever you happen to be, so you don't have to carry a cumbersome piece of work around with you.

Though the throw pictured has been made in a single main color, you could make squares from different shades of yarn and join them together for a multicolored effect.

WORKING IN THE ROUND

Instead of being worked in rows, some patterns start with a center ring and continue outward in rounds. When "working in the round," you stay on the right side at all times. This technique is used to make small, flat motifs and shaped items such as bags and hats.

MOTIFS

For the motif patterns on pages 54–55, unless otherwise specified:

- *Close the foundation chain ring by working a slip stitch into the first chain.*
- *At the beginning of each round work a turning chain to stand as the first stitch of the first pattern repeat (see the table on page 16 for the length of turning chains).*
- *At the end of each round close with a slip stitch into the top of this first stitch.*
- *Do not turn between rounds—right side is always facing.*

To create a flat item, increase regularly in each round. If you increase too much or too little, the fabric will curl or ripple. Shaped items like hats and bags are made with increases and decreases that force the item to cup or flare.

A flat piece made in the round may be any shape or pattern depending upon the position of the increases. Many different motifs are made using this technique (see pages 54–55). An enormous number of patchwork-style fabrics can be made by joining motifs together.

A tubular item like this tote bag (page 60) begins with a central foundation ring on the bottom. Increases give the bag its shape.

FOUNDATION RING

Working in the round starts with a foundation ring; the one most often used is closed by working a slip stitch into the first chain (chain foundation ring). When you want to be able to close any central hole in the fabric, use a yarn loop foundation ring.

CHAIN FOUNDATION RING

Make a short length of foundation chain as stated in the pattern instructions, for example, chain (ch) 5. Insert the hook into the first ch (left). Close the ring with a slip stitch (sl st) (right).

YARN LOOP FOUNDATION RING

Make a loop in the yarn. Hold the bottom of the loop with the fingers which normally hold the work. Insert the hook through the loop, wrap the yarn round the hook (left) and draw through. Make the correct turning chain (chain 1 for single crochet) and work the first round into the loop ring, making sure you encase the short end of yarn (right). Close the round with a sl st. Close up the center of the ring by drawing the short end of the yarn tight. Secure it by weaving it into the wrong side of the work.

WORKING IN JOINED ROUNDS

There are two ways to work in the round: making one continuous spiral or a series of joined rounds. In the latter case, each round is completed and joined with a slip stitch. Before starting the next round, a turning chain (t-ch) is made to match the height of the following stitches (even if the work is not turned between rounds). For the turning chain table see page 16.

1 *Make a foundation ring then work the correct number of chains for the t-ch, for example, ch 4 for triple (tr).*

2 *Insert the hook into the center of the foundation ring; work stitches as required for first round.*

3 *To close the round, work a slip stitch into the top of the turning chain.*

4 *Before working another round, make the required t-ch.*

DOUBLE CROCHET CLUSTER HEXAGON

Foundation ring: With A, ch 6. Work 1 round each in colors A, B, C, D, and E; join new yarn in ch sp.

Round 1: [Dc3tog in ring, ch 3] 6 times.

Round 2: [(Dc3tog, ch 3, dc3tog) in ch-3 sp, ch 3] 6 times.

Round 3: Join C in ch-3 sp, linking 2 pairs of cls, [(dc3tog, ch 3, dc3tog) in ch-3 sp, ch 3, dc3tog in next sp, ch 3] 6 times.

Round 4: Join D in ch-3 sp between 1st pair of cls, [(3 dc, ch 2, 3dc) in ch-3 sp, (3 dc in next ch-3 sp) twice] 6 times.

Round 5: Join E in ch-3 sp, [2 sc in ch-3 sp, 12 sc] 6 times.

POPCORN DIAMOND SQUARE

Foundation ring: Ch 8.

Special abbreviation pop (popcorn): 5 dc (see page 67).

Round 1: [1 pop, ch 5] 4 times.

Round 2: [1 dc, (2 dc, ch 2, 1 pop, ch 2, 2 dc) in ch-5 loop] 4 times.

Round 3: [3 dc, 2 dc in ch-2 sp, ch 2, 1 pop, ch 2, 2 dc in ch-2 sp, 2 dc] 4 times.

Round 4: [5 dc, 2 dc in ch-2 sp, ch 2, 1 pop, ch 2, 2 dc in ch-2 sp, 4 dc] 4 times.

SPIKED MEDALLION

Foundation ring: With A, ch 6.

Worked in colors A and B.

Special abbreviations scsp2 (spike single crochet 2 rounds below): Insert hook 2 rounds below st indicated, i.e. into top of round 1, yo, draw loop through and up to height of current round, yo, draw through both loops on hook (see Spikes, page 31).

pc (picot): Ch 3, sl st in sc first worked.

Round 1: With A, 16 sc in ring.

Round 2: With B, [2 sc, (1 sc, ch 9, 1 sc) in next, 1 sc] 4 times.

Round 3: [1 sc, skip 2 sc, (2 hdc, 17 dc, 2 hdc) in ch-9 arch, skip 2 sc] 4 times.

Round 4: Rejoin A in sc, [1 scsp2, ch 5, skip 5, 1 sc, 1 pc, (ch 5, skip 4, 1 sc, 1 pc) twice, ch 5, skip 5] 4 times.

FLOWER WHEEL

Foundation ring: Ch 5.

Round 1: 12 sc in ring.

Round 2: [2 dc, ch 3] 6 times.

Round 3: Sl st in dc and in next ch, [(dc3tog, ch 4, dc3tog) in ch sp, ch 4] 6 times.

Round 4: [(2sc, ch 3, 2 sc) in ch sp] 12 times.

GRANNY SQUARE

Foundation ring: With A, ch 4. Work 1 round each in colors A, B, C, and D; join new yarn in 2 ch sp.

Round 1: [3 dc in ring, ch 2] 4 times.

Round 2: [(3 dc, ch 2, 3 dc) in ch-2 sp, ch 1] 4 times.

Round 3: [(3 dc, ch 2, 3 dc) in ch-2 sp, ch 1, 3 dc in next sp, ch 1] 4 times.

Round 4: [(3 dc, ch 2, 3 dc) in ch-2 sp, (ch 1, 3 dc in next sp) twice, ch 1] 4 times.

FLOWER POWER

Foundation ring: Ch 6.

Round 1: 12 dc in ring.

Round 2: [1 sc, ch 7, skip 1] 5 times, 1 sc, ch 3, skip 1, 1 tr in top of first sc (counts as 6th ch-7 loop).

Round 3: [5 dc in ch loop, ch 3] 6 times.

Round 4: [5 dc, ch 3, 1 sc in ch loop, ch 3] 6 times.

Round 5: [Dc5tog, (ch 5, 1 sc in next loop) twice, ch 5] 6 times.

Round 6: Sl st in each of next 3 ch, [1 sc in ch loop, ch 5] 18 times.

Round 7: Sl st in each of next 3 ch, [1 sc in ch loop, ch 5, 1 sc in ch loop, ch 3, (5 dc, ch 3, 5 dc) in ch loop, ch 3] 6 times.

RAISED DOUBLE CROCHET SQUARE

Foundation ring: With A, ch 8. Work 1 round each in colors A, B, C, and D; join new yarn in ch-3 sp.

Round 1: [3 dc in ring, ch 3] 4 times.

Round 2: [3 dc in same sp, 3 rfdc, 3 dc in next sp, ch 3] 4 times.

Round 3: [3 dc in same sp, 3 rbdc, 3 rfdc, 3 rbdc, 3 dc in next sp, ch 3] 4 times.

Round 4: [3 dc in same sp, (3 rfdc, 3 rbdc) twice, 3 rfdc, 3 dc in next sp, ch 3] 4 times.

ROSE SQUARE

Foundation ring: With A, ch 6. Worked in colors A, B, and C.

Round 1: With A, 16 sc in ring.

Round 2: [1 dc, ch 3, skip 1 sc] 8 times.

Round 3: [Work a petal of (1 sc, 1 hdc, 5 dc, 1 hdc, 1 sc) in ch-3 sp] 8 times.

Round 4: With B, [1 sc between 2 sc, ch 6 behind petal of round 3] 8 times.

Round 5: [Work a petal of (1 sc, 1 hdc, 6 dc, 1 hdc, 1 sc) in ch-6 loop] 8 times.

Round 6: Join C in 2nd dc of petal of round 5, [1 sc in 2nd dc of petal, ch 6, skip 2, 1 sc, ch 6, skip 6] 8 times, omitting last 3 ch and working 1 dc in first sc of round instead to close round (counts as last ch-6 loop).

Round 7: [4 dc in same loop, ch 4, 1 sc in next loop, (ch 6, 1 sc in next loop) twice, ch 4, 4 dc in next loop, ch 4] 4 times.

PUFF STAR SQUARE

Foundation ring: Ch 4.

Special abbreviation puff: hdc4tog in same place (see page 67).

Round 1: 12 dc in ring.

Round 2: [1 puff, (ch 1, 1 puff) twice, ch 5] 4 times, close round with sl st, sl st in next ch sp.

Round 3: [1 puff in ch sp, ch 1, 1 puff in next ch sp, ch 2, 5 dc in ch-5 loop, ch 2] 4 times, close round with sl st, sl st in next ch sp.

Round 4: [1 puff in ch sp, ch 3, skip (1 puff, 2 ch), (1 dc, ch 1) twice, 5 dc in next, (ch 1, 1 dc) twice, ch 3, skip (2 ch, 1 puff)] 4 times, close round with sl st.

Round 5: 1 sc in each ch sp and each st around, except 3 sc in 3rd of 5 dc at each corner.

SPIRAL HEXAGON

Foundation ring: Ch 5.

Note: This motif is worked as a continuous spiral without joining between rounds. Hint: mark the last sc of each round with contrasting thread.

Round 1: [Ch 6, 1 sc in ring] 6 times.

Round 2: [Ch 4, 1 sc in next sp] 6 times.

Round 3: [Ch 4, 1 sc in next sp, 1 sc in next sc] 6 times.

Round 4: [Ch 4, 1 sc in next sp, 2 sc] 6 times.

Round 5: [Ch 4, 1 sc in next sp, 3 sc] 6 times.

Rep for as many rounds as desired, increasing number of sc in each of 6 sections of each round as established. From round 10 work 5 instead of 4 ch in each sp. End with a ch sp then 1 sl st in next sc.

ADULT BUCKET HAT

These summer hats are colorful, fun, and comfortable—and very

quick and easy to crochet.

❖ SIZE
One size: 22½" (57 cm)
circumference, to fit average head

❖ MATERIALS
Yarn Cotton glacé 100% cotton,
2 x 50 g balls
Hooks One size C crochet hook

❖ GAUGE
22 sts and 22 rows = 4" (10 cm)

❖ SKILLS USED
Chain (ch), p11; slip stitch (sl st),
p11; single crochet (sc), p13;
increasing, p21; working in the
round, p53

See pages 24–25 for pattern
abbreviations.

BABY BUCKET HAT

Make a miniature version for a baby you love—perfect for keeping

the sun off delicate skin.

❖ SIZE
One size: 17¾" (45 cm)
circumference, to fit average head

❖ MATERIALS
Yarn Sport weight cotton,
1 x 50 g ball
Hooks One size C crochet hook
Notions 12" (30 cm) of narrow
ribbon

❖ GAUGE
24 sts and 21 rows = 4" (10 cm)

❖ SKILLS USED
Chain (ch), p11; slip stitch (sl st),
p11; single crochet (sc), p13;
increasing, p21; working in the
round, p53; picots, p73

See pages 24–25 for pattern
abbreviations.

ADULT HAT

Using cotton glacé and size C hook, ch 6 and join with a sl st to form a foundation ring.

Round 1: Ch 2, 11 sc in ring, join with a sl st to 2nd ch of first ch (12 sc).

Round 2: Ch 2, 1 sc in 1st sc; *2 sc in each sc, rep from * to end; join with a sl st to 2nd ch of first ch (24 sc).

Round 3: Ch 2, 2 sc in next sc, *1 sc, 2 sc in next sc, rep from * to end; join with a sl st to 2nd ch of first ch (36 sc).

Round 4: Ch 2, 1 sc, 2 sc in next sc, *2 sc, 2 sc in next sc, rep from * to end join with a sl st to 2nd ch of first ch (48 sc).

Round 5: Ch 2, then continue in sc without shaping.

Round 6: Ch 2, 2 sc, 2 sc in next sc, *3 sc, 2 sc in next sc, rep from * to end join with a sl st to 2nd ch of first ch (60 sc).

Round 7: Ch 2, 3 sc, 2 sc in next sc, *4 sc, 2 sc in next sc, rep from * to end; join with a sl st to 2nd ch of first ch (72 sc).

Round 8: Ch 2, then continue in sc without shaping.

Round 9: Ch 2, 4 sc, 2 sc in next sc, *5 sc, 2 sc in next sc, rep from * to end join with a sl st to 2nd ch of first ch (84 sc).

Round 10: Ch 2, 5 sc, 2 sc in next sc, *6 sc, 2 sc in next sc, rep from * to end; join with a sl st to 2nd ch of first ch (96 sc).

Round 11: Ch 2, then continue in sc without shaping.

Round 12: Ch 2, 6 sc, 2 sc in next sc, *7 sc, 2 sc in next sc, rep from * to end; join with a sl st to 2nd ch of first ch (108 sc).

Round 13: Ch 2, 7 sc, 2 sc in next sc, *8 sc, 2 sc in next sc, rep from * to end; join with a sl st to 2nd ch of first ch (120 sc).

Round 14: Ch 2, then continue in sc without shaping.

Round 15: Ch 2, 8 sc, 2 sc in next sc, *9 sc, 2 sc in next sc, rep from * to end; join with a sl st to 2nd ch of first ch (132 sc).

Sides: Work 23 rounds in sc without shaping.

Shape brim: Ch 2, 9 sc, 2 sc in next sc, *10 sc, 2 sc in next sc, rep from * to end; join with a sl st to 2nd ch of first ch (144 sc).

Next round: Ch 2, 10 sc, 2 sc in next sc, *11 sc, 2 sc in next sc, rep from * to end; join with a sl st to 2nd ch of first ch (156 sc).

Next round: Ch 2, 11 sc, 2 sc in next sc, *12 sc, 2 sc in next sc, rep from * to end; join with a sl st to 2nd ch of first ch (168 sc).

Next round: Ch 2, 12 sc, 2 sc in next sc, *13 sc, 2 sc in next sc, rep from * to end; join with a sl st to 2nd ch of first ch (180 sc).

FINISHING

Pin or stitch crochet flowers to the hat for an extra flourish. See pages 92–93 for instructions on how to make flowers.

BABY HAT

Using sport weight yarn and size C hook, proceed in exactly the same way as the adult hat, up to and including Round 12 (108 sc).

Work 20 rounds in sc without shaping.

Next round: Ch 2, 7 sc, 2 sc in next sc, *8 sc, 2 sc in next sc, rep from * to end; join with a sl st to 2nd ch of first ch (120 sc).

Next round: Ch 2, 8 sc, 2 sc in next sc, *9 sc, 2 sc in next sc, rep from * to end; join with a sl st to 2nd ch of first ch (132 sc).

Next round: Ch 2, 9 sc, 2 sc in next sc, *10 sc, 2 sc in next sc), rep from * to end; join with a sl st to 2nd ch of first ch (144 sc).

Next round (picot edge): (Ch 4, sl st into same sc, sl st into next 2 sc) 48 times; fasten off.

FINISHING

Turn back brim, push ends of ribbon through from inside, between stitches, and tie in a bow.

MULTICOLORED BAG

This everyday bag is made from hand-dyed cotton yarn that creates a striped look. Instructions on how to dye your own yarn can be found on page 94.

❖ SIZES
8" (20 cm) long

❖ MATERIALS
Yarn *Very fine (12-gauge) cotton,*
1 x 50 g ball
Hooks *One size 6 steel crochet*
hook

❖ GAUGE
33 sts and 30 rows = 4" (10 cm)

❖ SKILLS USED
Chain (ch), p11; slip stitch (sl st),
p11; single crochet (sc), p13;
double crochet (dc), p15;
increasing, p21; working in the
round, p53; picots, p73

See page 24–25 for pattern
abbreviations.

BEADED BAG

This evening bag is embellished with iridescent glass beads. The top has a fluted, picot edge worked in a double layer. Beads are threaded onto the yarn and worked into the stitches as they are formed.

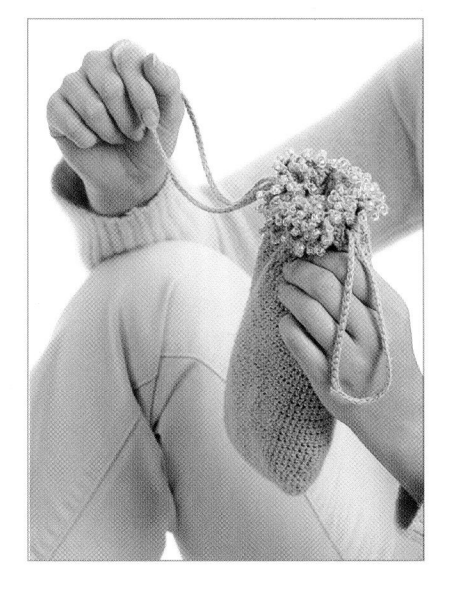

❖ SIZES
9" (22.5 cm) long

❖ MATERIALS
Yarn *Sport weight cotton,*
1 x 50 g ball
Hooks *One size C crochet hook*
Notions *90 beads, approximately*
5 mm diameter

❖ GAUGE
24 sts and 21 rows = 4" (10 cm)

❖ SKILLS USED
Chain (ch), p11; slip stitch (sl st),
p11; single crochet (sc), p13;
double crochet (dc), p15;
increasing, p21; working in the
round, p53; picots, p73

See page 24–25 for pattern
abbreviations.

MULTICOLORED BAG

Worked in the round, in one piece, starting from the base.

Using the fine yarn and size 6 steel hook, ch 6, join with sl st in first ch to form ring.

Round 1: Ch 2, 11 sc in ring, join with a sl st to 2nd ch of ch-2 (12 sc).

Round 2: Ch 2, 1 sc in next sc, *2 sc in next sc, rep from * to end; join with a sl st to 2nd ch of ch-2 (24 sc).

Round 3: Ch 2, 2 sc in next sc, *1 sc, 2 sc in next sc, rep from * to end; join with a sl st to 2nd ch of ch-2 (36 sc).

Round 4: Ch 2, 1 sc, 2 sc in next sc, *2 sc, 2 sc in next sc, rep from * to end; join with a sl st to 2nd ch of ch-2 (48 sc).

Round 5: Ch 2, 2 sc, 2 sc in next sc, *3 sc, 2 sc in next sc, rep from * to end; join with a sl st to 2nd ch of ch-2 (60 sc).

Round 6: Ch 2, 3 sc, 2 sc in next sc, *4 sc, 2 sc in next sc, rep from * to end; join with a sl st to 2nd ch of ch-2 (72 sc).

Round 7: Ch 2, 4 sc, 2 sc in next sc, *5 sc, 2 sc in next sc, rep from * to end; join with a sl st to 2nd ch of ch-2 (84 sc).

Work 50 rounds in sc without shaping.

Next round (eyelets): Ch 3, 1 dc in next sc, *ch 1, skip 1 sc, 2 dc, repeat from * to end, ch 1, join with a sl st to 3rd ch of ch-3. Work 1 round of sc without shaping.

Next round (picot edge): (Ch 4, sl st into same sc, sl st into next 2 sc) 28 times; fasten off.

CORDS

Using the fine yarn and size 6 steel hook, ch 100, turn and work sc all along chain to end; fasten off. Repeat to make a second cord.

FINISHING

Thread one of the cords in and out of the eyelets and join the ends. Starting on the opposite side of the bag from where the first cords emerge, thread the remaining cord through the eyelets and join the ends.

BEADED BAG

Worked in the round, in one piece, starting from the base.

Using sport weight cotton and size C hook, ch 20.

Round 1: Ch 2, 18 sc along foundation ch; 3 sc in last st, then work 19 sc back along opposite side of foundation ch, 3 sc in last st, join with a sl st to 2nd ch of ch-2 (44 sc).

Round 2: Ch 2, 19 sc, 3 sc in next sc, 21 sc, 3 sc in next sc, 1 sc; join with a sl st to 2nd ch of ch-2 (48 sc).

Round 3: Ch 2, 20 sc, 3 sc in next sc, 23 sc, 3 sc in next sc, 2 sc; join with a sl st to 2nd ch of ch-2 (52 sc).

Round 4: Ch 2, 21 sc, 3 sc in next sc, 25 sc, 3 sc in next sc, 3 sc; join with a sl st to 2nd ch of ch-2 (56 sc).

Round 5: Ch 2, 22 sc, 3 sc in next sc, 27 sc, 3 sc in next sc, 4 sc; join with a sl st to 2nd ch of ch-2 (60 sc).

Work 30 rounds in sc without shaping.

Next round (increase): Ch 2, 2 sc in next sc, *1 sc, 2 sc in next sc, repeat from * to end; join with a sl st to 2nd ch of ch-2 (90 sc).

Work 5 rounds in sc without shaping.

Next round (eyelets): **Ch 4, 1 dc in next sc, *ch 1, skip 1 sc, 1 dc in next sc, repeat from * to end, 1 ch, join with a sl st to 3nd ch of ch-4.

Work 1 row of sc. Fasten off yarn. Thread beads onto ball of yarn and rejoin yarn to edge of work.

Next round (picot edge): *Ch 2, slip one bead along yarn, close to last stitch worked, ch 2, sl st into base of picot, sl st into next 2 sc, repeat from * to end (45 times in total—i.e. 45 picots, each with a single bead) and fasten off.

Rejoin yarn to work 1 row below eyelet row, work 1 row of sc, then repeat from ** to make the second layer of the double-layered edging.

CORDS

Using sport weight cotton and size C hook, ch 100, turn and work sc all along chain to end; fasten off. Repeat to make a second cord.

FINISHING

Thread the cords in and out through both layers of eyelets, as in the multicolored bag.

TUBULAR TOTE

Here is a practical, go-anywhere, take-anything bag. It features bold stripes and is worked in the round.

 SIZE
One size: 12" (30 cm) long and 26" (65.5 cm) around

✤ **MATERIALS**
Yarn Cotton glacé 100% cotton, 2 x 50 g balls color A,
1 x 50 g ball color B, 2 x 50 g balls color C
Hook One size D crochet hook

✤ **GAUGE**
22 sts and 22 rows = 4" (10 cm)

✤ **SKILLS USED**
Chain (ch), p11; slip stitch (sl st), p11; single crochet (sc),
p13; increasing, p21; changing colors and rejoining yarn,
p39; working in the round, p53

See pages 24–25 for pattern abbreviations.

TUBULAR TOTE

Using color A and 3 mm hook, ch 6, join with sl st in first ch to form ring.

Round 1: Ch 2, 11 sc in ring, join with a sl st to 2nd ch of ch-2 (12 sc).

Round 2: Ch 2, 1 sc in 1st sc; *2 sc in each sc, rep from * to end; join with a sl st to 2nd ch of ch-2 (24 sc).

Round 3: Ch 2, 2 sc in next sc, *1 sc, 2 sc in next sc, rep from * to end; join with a sl st to 2nd ch of ch-2 (36 sc).

Round 4: Ch 2, 1 sc, 2 sc in next sc, *2 sc, 2 sc in next sc, rep from * to end join with a sl st to 2nd ch of ch-2 (48 sc).

Round 5: Ch 2, then continue in sc without shaping.

Round 6: Ch 2, 2 sc, 2 sc in next sc, *3 sc, 2 sc in next sc, rep from * to end join with

COLORWAYS

This tote bag has been made in light, clean colors—just right for summer days. For a change of mood, why not pick some hot bright reds and pinks—maybe teamed with a zingy yellow? Alternatively, go for more muted shades—earthy browns and leafy greens—and give your bag a more autumnal feel. And if you can't find the color you want, try dyeing yarn to the shade of your choice (see page 94).

a sl st to 2nd ch of ch-2 (60 sc).

Round 7: Ch 2, 3 sc, 2 sc in next sc, *4 sc, 2 sc in next sc, rep from * to end; join with a sl st to 2nd ch of ch-2 (72 sc).

Round 8: Ch 2, then continue in sc without shaping.

Round 9: Ch 2, 4 sc, 2 sc in next sc, *5 sc, 2 sc in next sc, rep from * to end join with a sl st to 2nd ch of ch-2 (84 sc).

Round 10: Ch 2, 5 sc, 2 sc in next sc, *6 sc, 2 sc in next sc, rep from * to end; join with a sl st to 2nd ch of ch-2 (96 sc).

Round 11: Ch 2, then continue in sc without shaping.

Round 12: Ch 2, 6 sc, 2 sc in next sc, *7 sc, 2 sc in next sc, rep from * to end; join with a sl st to 2nd ch of ch-2 (108 sc).

Round 13: Ch 2, 7 sc, 2 sc in next sc, *8 sc, 2 sc in next sc, rep from * to end; join with a sl st to 2nd ch of ch-2 (120 sc).

Round 14: Ch 2, then continue in sc without shaping.

Round 15: Ch 2, 8 sc, 2 sc in next sc, *9 sc, 2 sc in next sc, rep from * to end; join with a sl st to 2nd ch of ch-2 (132 sc).

Round 16: Ch 2, 9 sc, 2 sc in next sc, *10 sc, 2 sc in next sc, rep from * to end; join with a sl st to 2nd ch of ch-2 (144 sc). Work 25 rounds without shaping; fasten off yarn.

Next round: Join in color B and work 3 rounds without shaping; turn, and work 8 rounds; turn and work 10 rounds (this forms a textured stripe in the center of the bag); fasten off yarn.

Next round: Join in color C and work 30 rounds; do not fasten off yarn but start to make first handle: Ch 100, count 20 sts along top of bag and sl st to next st. Work back along ch, working 1 sc into each ch; sl st in sc next to 1st ch, then work back along handle again, working 1 sc in each sc of previous row; sl st to top of bag, then work 1 sl st in each of 26 sts along top edge of bag, to take you to the position where you begin the 2nd handle. Work the 2nd handle in the same way as the first; fasten off yarn.

HANDLES

Make handles shorter or longer, according to your needs, or simply work one wide shoulder strap from one side of the bag to the other, if you prefer.

PET BASKET WITH LINER

Sturdy but soft, this basket will become the favorite retreat of your

cat or small dog. The washable liner is crocheted with fabric strips

you cut from an old T-shirt.

❖ SIZE
One size: 13½" (34 cm) diameter, 6" (15 cm) high

❖ MATERIALS
Yarn Utility string, about 220 yds (200 m)
Plus One old T-shirt, cut into ½" (12 mm) strips
[see Making fabric strips, page 63]
Hooks One each size J and size K crochet hooks

❖ GAUGE
10 sts and 11 rows = 4" (10 cm)

❖ SKILLS USED
Chain (ch), p11; slip stitch (sl st), p11; single crochet (sc),
p13; increasing, p21; changing colors and rejoining yarn,
p39; working in the round, p53

See pages 24–25 for pattern abbreviations.

PET BASKET WITH LINER

Note: the basket and the liner are each worked in one piece, in the round.

BASE

Using utility string and size J hook, ch 6, join with sl st in first ch to form ring.

Round 1: Ch 2, 11 sc in ring, join with a sl st to 2nd ch of ch-2 (12 sc).

Round 2: Ch 2, 1 sc in 1st sc; 2 sc in each sc; join with a sl st to 2nd ch of ch-2 (24 sc).

Round 3: Ch 2, 2 sc in next sc, [1 sc, 2 sc in next sc] 11 times; join with a sl st to 2nd ch of ch-2 (36 sc).

Round 4: Work 1 round in sc without shaping.

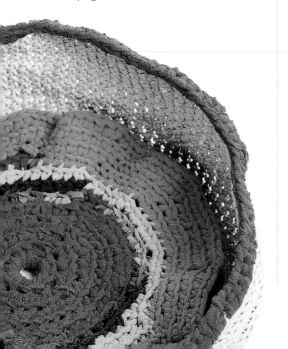

Round 5: Ch 2, 2 sc in next sc, [2 sc, 2 sc in next sc] 11 times, 1 sc; join with a sl st to 2nd ch of ch-2 (48 sc).

Round 6: Ch 2, 2 sc in next sc, [3 sc, 2 sc in next sc] 11 times, 2 sc; join with a sl st to 2nd ch of ch-2 (60 sc).

Round 7: Work 1 round in sc without shaping.

Round 8: Ch 2, 2 sc in next sc, [4 sc, 2 sc in next sc] 11 times, 3 sc; join with a sl st to 2nd ch of ch-2 (72 sc).

Round 9: Work 1 round in sc without shaping.

Round 10: Ch 2, 2 sc in next sc, [5 sc, 2 sc in next sc] 11 times, 4 sc; join with a sl st to 2nd ch of ch-2 (84 sc).

Round 11: Work 1 round in sc without shaping.

Round 12: Ch 2, 2 sc in next sc, [6 sc, 2 sc in next sc] 11 times, 5 sc; join with a sl st to 2nd ch of ch-2 (96 sc).

Round 13: Work 1 round in sc without shaping.

Round 14: Ch 2, 2 sc in next sc, [7 sc, 2 sc in next sc] 11 times, 6 sc; join with a sl st to 2nd ch of ch-2 (108 sc).

SIDES

Turn and work 14 rounds without shaping.

Next round: Ch 3, 1 sc in next sc, *ch 1 skip 1 sc, 1 sc in next sc, repeat from * to end; join with a sl st to 2nd ch of ch-3; fasten off yarn.

BORDER

Join in fabric strip; ch 2, 1 sc into 1st ch sp; *2 sc into next 1 ch sp, repeat from * to end; fasten off.

LINER

Note: As you come to the end of one fabric strip, join in another of the same or a different color.

Using fabric strips and size K hook, ch 6, join with sl st in first ch to form ring.

Round 1: Ch 2, 11 sc in ring, join with a sl st to 2nd ch of ch-2 (12 sc).

Round 2: Ch 2, 1 sc in 1st sc; 2 sc in each sc; join with a sl st to 2nd ch of ch-2 (24 sc).

Round 3: Ch 2, 2 sc in next sc, [1 sc, 2 sc in next sc] 11 times; join with a sl st to 2nd ch of ch-2 (36 sc).

Round 4: Ch 2, 2 sc in next sc, [2 sc, 2 sc in next sc] 11 times, 1 sc; join with a sl st to 2nd ch of ch-2 (48 sc).

Round 5: Ch 2, 2 sc in next sc, [3 sc, 2 sc in next sc] 11 times, 2 sc; join with a sl st to 2nd ch of ch-2 (60 sc).

Round 6: Ch 2, 2 sc in next sc, [4 sc, 2 sc in next sc] 11 times, 3 sc; join with a sl st to 2nd ch of ch-2 (72 sc).

Round 7: Ch 2, 2 sc in next sc, [5 sc, 2 sc in next sc] 11 times, 4 sc; join with a sl st to 2nd ch of ch-2 (84 sc).

Round 8: Ch 2, 2 sc in next sc, [6 sc, 2 sc in next sc] 11 times, 5 sc; join with a sl st to 2nd ch of ch-2 (96 sc).

Round 9: Ch 2, 2 sc in next sc, [7 sc, 2 sc

MAKING FABRIC STRIPS FROM OLD T-SHIRTS

This can be done so that you end up with one long, continuous strip. First cut off T-shirt hem and discard, then, beginning at one of the side seams, start to cut around the body of the garment, ½" (12 mm) from the raw edge. When you reach the starting point, do not cut off the strip you have made but continue cutting in a spiral around the garment until you reach the armholes, then snip off.

in next sc] 11 times, 6 sc; join with a sl st to 2nd ch of ch-2 (108 sc).

Round 10: Ch 2, 2 sc in next sc, [8 sc, 2 sc in next sc] 11 times, 7 sc; join with a sl st to 2nd ch of ch-2 (120 sc).

Round 11: Ch 2, 2 sc in next sc, [9 sc, 2 sc in next sc] 11 times, 8 sc; join with a sl st to 2nd ch of ch-2 (132 sc).

Round 12: Ch 2, 2 sc in next sc, [10 sc, 2 sc in next sc] 11 times, 9 sc; join with a sl st to 2nd ch of ch-2 (144 sc).

GRANNY SQUARE TOP

Granny squares are back! This patchwork top is pieced together from individual squares, opening up many possibilities for combining colors. You could try other square motifs from pages 54 and 55; just adjust your hook size if necessary to get the correct measurements.

❖ **SIZE**

One size: To fit 34–36" (86–91 cm) bust. Finished size 38" (96 cm) around bust and 20" (50 cm) from shoulder to hem

❖ **MATERIALS**

Yarn Sport weight 100% cotton, 1 x 50 g ball color A (yellow), 3 x 50 g balls color B (pink), 3 x 50 g balls color C (green). Cotton glacé 4 x 50 g balls color D (blue)
Hook One size C crochet hook
Notions Tapestry needle, buttons (pink, blue, and yellow)

❖ **GAUGE**

1 square = 3¾" (9 cm) approx

❖ **SKILLS USED**

Chain (ch), p11; slip stitch (sl st), p11; double crochet (dc), p15; joining seams, p27; changing colors and rejoining yarn, p39; working in the round, p52–5

See pages 24–25 for pattern abbreviations.

GRANNY SQUARE TOP

Note: At beginning of every round, work ch 3 in place of 1st dc.

MAKING A GRANNY SQUARE

Using color A and size C hook, ch 5 and join with a sl st to form a foundation ring.

Round 1: (3 dc in ring, ch 2) 4 times; join with sl st to 3rd ch of ch-3). Break off yarn.

Round 2: Join in color B in any ch-2 sp. [(3 dc, ch-2, 3 dc) in ch-2 sp, ch 1] 4 times. Break off yarn.

Round 3: Join in color C in any ch-2 sp. [(3 dc, ch 2, 3 dc) in ch-2 sp, ch 1, 2 dc in ch-1 sp, ch 1] 4 times. Break off yarn.

Round 4: Join in color D in any ch-2 sp. [(3 dc, ch 2, 3 dc) in ch-2 sp, (ch 1, 2 dc in ch-1 sp) twice, ch 1] 4 times. Break off yarn. Make 47 more squares in this way. Using a tapestry needle and length of color D, stitch 10 squares together in a row. Repeat this three more times then stitch the four rows together to make the body. Add two rows of four to make the straps.

FINISHING

Join in color B at front lower right corner in ch-2 sp. Work border: (3 dc, ch 2, 3 dc) in ch-2 sp, [(ch 1, 2 dc in next sp), ch 1] 18 times, (3 dc, ch 2, 3 dc) in ch-2 sp. This forms the border for the right front (buttonhole) edge. Continue in the same manner, around the neck edge, over the right strap, across the back, over the left strap, down the left front and around the lower hem, in exactly the same way, working (3 dc, ch 2, 3 dc) in ch-2 sp at outer corners. When you get to an inner corner, skip one of the ch-2 sp (at the corner of the square motif) and simply work 2 dc in the next ch-2 sp, on the adjacent square. Work a similar border around each armhole.

Sew buttons, evenly spaced down left front edge, and aligned with holes in border on opposite edge, which act as buttonholes.

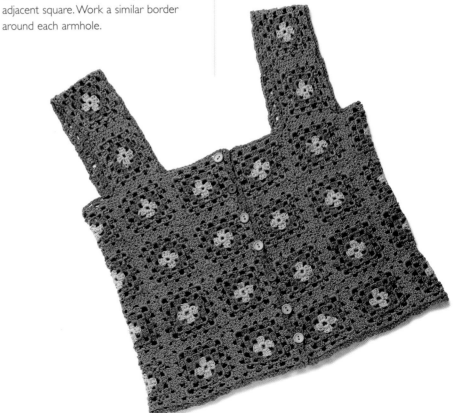

DOG COAT

Make a matching coat for your dog—a kind of pooch poncho! Sizes will vary, according to the size of your dog, but use the one pictured as a guide. Join rows of squares to achieve the size and shape you desire, then add straps to fasten under the tummy and around the chest.

RELIEF EFFECT STITCHES

A relief stitch sticks out from the surface, creating texture. Popcorn stitch, puff stitch, bobbles, and bullion stitch are examples of relief stitches. They are easy to crochet because they use the same skills as increasing and decreasing.

A relief effect is created whenever you work a stitch taller than the stitches on either side—for example, a triple crochet in a row of single crochet. The taller stitch cannot lie flat, but sticks out from the surface.

Similarly, if you work more than one stitch into the same place and then join the group into a stitch at the top, the excess will stand out. The taller and greater the number of stitches in the cluster, the more pronounced the bobble will be. Variations can be made using different numbers of stitches and inserting the hook in different positions.

This hat uses raised bobbles to add texture and interest (see page 70).

POPCORN STITCH

1 Work 5 stitches into the same place. Remove the hook from the working loop.

2 Insert it from front to back under the top 2 loops of the first stitch in the group. Pick up the working loop again and draw it through. To make a popcorn stitch stand out toward the back of the work, insert hook from back through to front.

PUFF STITCH

1 Work a cluster of half double crochet (hdc). Wrap the yarn round the hook (yo), insert hook into stitch (st), yo, draw loop through loosely. Without tightening the other loops on the hook, repeat 4 times.

2 Yo and draw through all loops on hook. To secure, leave last of 11 loops on hook, yo and draw through the remaining 2 loops.

BOBBLE

1 Work a decrease cluster of 5 double crochet (dc) (or whatever amount you like) all into the same place, in a row made otherwise of single crochet (sc). *Wrap the yarn round the hook (yo), insert hook into stitch (st), yo, draw a loop through, yo, draw through 2 loops; repeat from * 4 more times always inserting hook into same st (6 loops on hook).

2 Yo and draw yarn through all loops to complete. The bobble is more pronounced when worked during wrong side rows.

BULLION STITCH

1 Wrap the yarn round the hook (yo) 6 or 7 times, as if making a long stitch (st). Insert hook, yo, and draw through st. Yo, draw through all the loops.

2 Allow enough yarn to be drawn through the loops to give them enough room to stand up as far as you wish. Yo once more and, taking care not to allow the stem of the bullion st to tighten, draw through to complete.

BOBBLE PANEL

Worked over 13 sts on a background of alt dc (right side) and sc rows.

Special abbreviation bob (bobble stitch): dc5tog in same place (see page 67).

Note: Work each rftr around dc st 2 rows below.

Row 1 (right side): 13 dc.

Row 2 (wrong side): 4 sc, 1 bob, 3 sc, 1 bob, 4 sc.

Row 3: 1 rftr, 1 dc, 1 rftr, 7 dc, 1 rftr, 1 dc, 1 rftr.

Row 4: 6 sc, 1 bob, 6 sc.

Row 5: As row 3.

Rows 2 to 5 form the pattern.

BULLION WAVES

Multiple of 10 sts plus 2, plus 1 for foundation ch.

Special abbreviation bst (bullion stitch): Made with (yo) 10 times (see page 67).

Note: 1-ch counts as stitch only on right side (bullion stitch) rows.

Row 1 (wrong side): Skip 1 ch, sc across, turn.

Row 2: Ch 3, *5 dc, 5 bsts; rep from * to last st, 1 dc, turn.

Row 3: Ch 1, sc across, turn.

Row 4: Ch 3, *5 bsts, 5 dc; rep from * to last st, 1 dc, turn.

Row 5: As row 3.

Rows 2 to 5 form the pattern.

CROSSED DOUBLE TRIPLE CABLE PANEL

Worked over 19 sts on a background of dc.

Note: See page 43 for crossed stitches.

Row 1 (wrong side): 19 dc.

Row 2 (right side): 1 rftr, 1 dc, skip 3, 3 dtr, going in back of last 3 dtr work 3 dtr in 3 skipped sts, 1 dc, 1 rftr, 1 dc, skip 3, 3 dtr, going in front of last 3 dtr but not encasing them, work 3 dtr in 3 skipped sts, 1 dc, 1 rftr.

Row 3 (wrong side): As row 1, except work rbtr instead of rftr over 1st, 10th, and 19th sts to keep raised ridges on right side of fabric.

Rows 2 and 3 form the pattern.

DOUBLE CROCHET BOBBLES

Multiple of 4 sts plus 1, plus 2 for foundation ch.

Row 1 (right side): Skip 3 ch, dc across, turn.

Row 2: Ch 1, 1 sc, *dc5tog in next, 3 sc; rep from * to last 3 sts, dc5tog in next, 2 sc, turn.

Row 3: Ch 3, dc across, turn.

Row 4: Ch 1, *3 sc, dc5tog in next; rep from * to last 4 sts, 4 sc, turn.

Row 5: As row 3.

Rows 2 to 5 form the pattern.

PUFFS AND RAISED CROSSES PANEL

Worked over 11 sts on a background of dc.

Special abbreviations puff (puff stitch): hdc5tog in same place (see page 67).

nc (not closed): see Clusters page 73.

Row 1 (right side): 11 dc.

Row 2 (wrong side): *1 rbtr, 1 puff, 1 rbtr**, 1 dc; rep from * once more and from * to ** again.

Row 3: *1 dcnc in first, skip puff, 1 rftrnc around next (3 loops on hook), yo, draw through all loops, 1 dc in puff, 1 dcnc in next, 1 rftrnc around st before previous puff crossing in front of previous rftr, yo, and draw through 3 loops as before**, 1 dc; rep from * once more and from * to ** again.

Rows 2 and 3 form the pattern.

DOUBLE BULLIONS

Multiple of 6 sts plus 2, plus 1 for foundation ch.

Special abbreviation bst (bullion stitch): Made with (yo) 7 times (see page 67).

Note: T-ch counts as stitch only on right side (bullion stitch) rows.

Row 1 (wrong side): Skip 1 ch, 1 sc, ch 1, skip 1 ch, 1 sc, * ch 2, skip 2 ch, 1 sc; rep from * to last ch-2 sp, ch 1, skip 1 ch, 1 sc, turn.

Row 2: Ch 3, 1 dc in ch sp, *1 dc, 2 bsts in ch-2 sp, 1 dc, 2 dc in ch-2 sp; rep from * across, working last dc in last sc, turn.

Row 3: Ch 1, 1 sc, ch 1, skip 1, 1 sc, *ch 2, skip 2, 1 sc; rep from * to last 2 sts, ch 1, skip 1, 1 sc, turn.

Row 4: Ch 3, 1 bst in next ch sp, *1 dc, 2 dc in next ch sp, 1 dc **, 2 bsts in ch-2 sp; rep from * to last 6 sts and from * to ** again, 1 bst in next ch sp, 1 dc, turn.

Row 5: As row 3.

Rows 2 to 5 form the pattern.

PUFFS AND SINGLE CROCHET

Multiple of 4 sts plus 1, plus 1 for foundation ch.

Special abbreviation puff (puff stitch): hdc4tog in same place (see page 67).

Row 1 (right side): Skip 2 ch, sc across, turn.

Row 2: Ch 1, 1 sc, *1 puff, 3 sc; rep from * across, omitting 1 sc at end of last rep, turn.

Row 3: Ch 1, sc across, turn.

Row 4: Ch 1, *3 sc, 1 puff; rep from * to last 4 sts, 4 sc, turn.

Row 5: As row 3.

Rows 2 to 5 form the pattern

POPCORNS AND DOUBLE CROCHET

Multiple of 6 sts plus 1, plus 2 for foundation ch.

Special abbreviation pop (popcorn stitch): 5 dc (see page 67).

Work 1 row each in colors A, B and C throughout.

Row 1 (right side): Skip 3 ch, dc across, turn.

Row 2: Ch 1 (does not count as st), *1 sc, ch 1, skip 1; rep from * to last st, 1 sc, turn.

Row 3: Ch 3, *skip (1 ch, 1 sc), (1 pop, ch 1, 1 dc, ch 1, 1 pop) in next ch sp, skip (1 sc, 1 ch), 1 dc; rep from * across, turn.

Row 4: As row 2.

Row 5: Ch 3, dc across, turn.

Rows 2 to 5 form the pattern

DIAGONAL SPIKE PUFF

Multiple of 3 sts plus 2, plus 2 for foundation ch.

Special abbreviation spfcl (spike puff cluster): Yo, insert hook in next st, yo, draw through, yo, draw through 2 loops, (yo, insert hook from front in 3rd previous st, yo, draw through loosely) twice (6 loops on hook), yo, draw through all loops.

Row 1 (right side): Skip 3 ch, *2 dc, 1 spfcl; rep from * to last st, 1 dc, turn.

Row 2: Ch 3, *2 dc, 1 spfcl; rep from * to last st, 1 dc, turn.

Row 2 forms the pattern.

VERTICAL POPCORNS WITH RAISED TRIPLES

Multiple of 11 sts plus 3, plus 2 for foundation ch.

Special abbreviation pop (popcorn stitch): 5 tr (see page 67).

Row 1 (right side): Skip 3 ch, 2 dc, *ch 2, skip 3 ch, 1 pop, ch 1, 1 pop, ch 1, skip 3 ch, 3 dc; rep from * across, turn.

Row 2: Ch 3, 1 rbtr, 1 dc, *ch 3, skip (1 ch, 1 pop), 2 sc in ch sp, ch 3, skip (1 pop, 2 ch), 1 dc, 1 rbtr, 1 dc; rep from * across, turn.

Row 3: Ch 3, 1 rftr, 1 dc, *ch 2, skip 3 ch, 1 pop, ch 1, 1 pop, ch 1, skip 3 ch, 1 dc, 1 rftr, 1 dc; rep from * across, turn.

Rows 2 and 3 form the pattern.

BOBBLE HAT

This hat in a tweedy yarn features a decorative bobble pattern that makes it look and feel chunky and warm.

❖ SIZE
One size: 23" (58 cm) circumference, to fit average head

❖ MATERIALS
***Yarn** Knitting worsted 100% pure new wool,
2 x 50 g balls*
***Hook** One size F crochet hook*
***Notions** Tapestry needle*

❖ GAUGE
16 sts and 9 rows = 4" (10 cm)

❖ SKILLS USED
*Chain (ch), p11; slip stitch (sl st), p11; double crochet
(dc), p15; double triple crochet (dtr), p15; increasing, p21;
working in the round, p53; bobble stitch (bob), p67*

See pages 24–25 for pattern abbreviations.

BOBBLE HAT

SPECIAL ABBREVIATION

Bob (bobble): dc5tog in next st

BOBBLE PATTERN

Round 1: Ch 1, 1 dc, ch 1, skip 1 dc, 2 dc, 1 bob, * 2 dc, ch 1, skip 1 dc, 2 dc, 1 bob; rep from * to end

Round 2: Ch 3, then continue in dc. These two rounds form the bobble pattern.

Note: The hat is made in one piece, starting from the center of the crown and working in the round.

COLORWAYS

You could work the hexagonal crown in one color, the bobble patterned sides in another and the rolled brim in another—a great way to use up leftover yarn from a larger project.

CROWN

Using knitting worsted and size F hook, ch 6 and join with sl st in first ch to form foundation ring.

Round 1: Ch 3, 2 dc into ring, *ch 3, 3 dc into ring, rep from * 4 times more, ch 3; join with a sl st to 3rd ch of first ch.

Round 2: Ch 5, (2 dtr, ch 2, 3 dtr) into first sp, *(3 dtr, ch 2, 3 dtr) into next sp, rep from * 4 times more, join with a sl st in 5th ch of first ch.

Round 3: Ch 3, 2 dc, *(2 dc, ch 2, 2 dc) into ch-2 sp, 6 dc, rep from * 4 times more, (2 dc, ch 2, 2 dc) into ch-2 sp, 3 dc, join with a sl st in 3rd ch of first ch.

Round 4: Ch 3, 4 dc, *(2 dc, ch 2, 2 dc) into ch-2 sp, 10 dc, rep from * 4 times more, (2 dc, ch 2, 2 dc) into ch-2 sp, 5 dc, join with a sl st in 3rd ch of first ch.

Round 5: Work 1 round of dc without any shaping (96 dc).

Now work 10 rounds following the bobble pattern, joining each round with a sl st in the 3rd ch of first ch.

BRIM

Work 9 further rounds of dc. Fasten off yarn.

FINISHING

Turn up the brim. Thread a tapestry needle with a length of the yarn and make a few small stitches around the brim, on the inside, to hold it in place.

SHELLS, CLUSTERS, AND LACE

Crochet can create delicate work that is also strong and durable. Stitches and crochet techniques can be combined to make different shapes and openwork patterns. Color changes can add to the finished effect.

You can make attractive patterns by grouping stitches together in shells or clusters. Shells are formed by working a group of stitches into the same place, whereas a cluster is made of several adjacent stitches joined together at the top. Work these closely together, or for a delicate look, increase the spacing. Combine shells and clusters with mesh techniques (see page 76–79) to create lacy work.

Use lacy effects in crochet to make garments with a light and delicate look (see page 74).

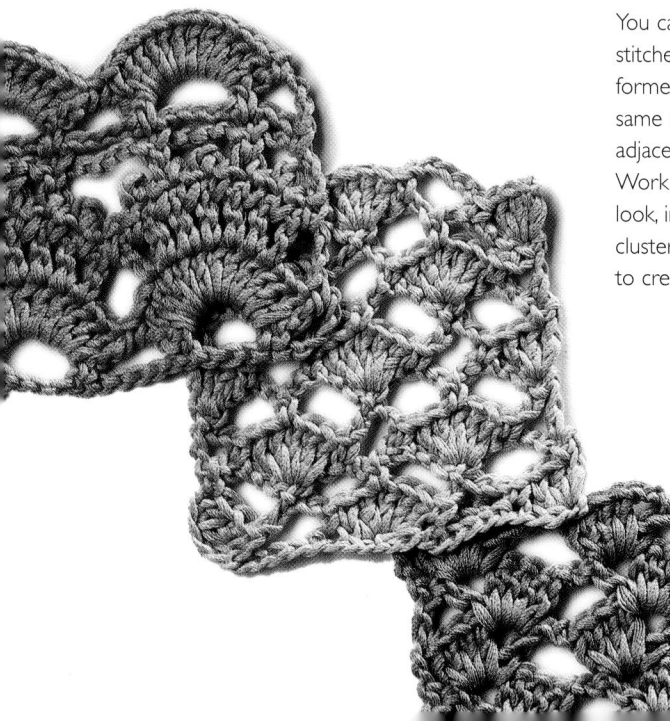

SHELLS

Shell shapes in crochet are made by working several stitches into one place. These stitches may be all the same, or of varying heights to create an asymmetric shape. Shells may also contain chains to create spaces. If no stitches are skipped, working more than one stitch into the same place will make an increase (see page 21). If groups of stitches are worked at intervals with other shells between them, no increase is created. See Interlocking Double Crochet Shells, page 44.

CLUSTERS

A cluster is a group of stitches worked into one stitch or space then drawn together at the top with a loop. A shell and a cluster in combination can make a starburst.

1 *Work the required number of stitches, leaving the last loop of each one on the hook. These are sometimes called not closed (nc).*

2 *Wrap the yarn round the hook (yo); draw the yarn through all the loops.*

LACE

Lacework consists of shells and clusters as well as meshes (see pages 76–79), single chains, and arches or loops, including picots. There are two ways of working over chains. In the first method, insert the hook in between the threads of a particular chain (see 1). In the second, insert the hook into the space underneath a chain or chain loop (see 2). The second method is quicker and easier, so use this unless otherwise instructed.

PICOTS

These single or multiple chain loops are anchored together for decoration. They are often featured in Irish crochet lace networks (see page 77), and are frequently used as edgings (see page 86). To make this simple picot (right) the instructions would be: *1 single crochet (sc) in chain (ch) space, (ch 3, slip stitch (sl st) in 3rd ch from hook—called picot).*

LACY CAMISOLE

This camisole has a timeless quality, with its lacy stitch, tiny pearl buttons and slim straps. Pair it with jeans for a trendy, casual look or with dressy pants for evening wear.

❖ SIZE

One size: To fit 34–36" (86–91 cm) bust. Finished size 37" (94 cm) around bust and 24" (61 cm) from shoulder to hem

❖ MATERIALS

Yarn *Sport weight 100% cotton, 3 x 50 g balls*
Hook *One size D crochet hook*
Notions *¼" (6 mm) mother-of-pearl buttons*

❖ GAUGE

12 rows = 4" (10 cm) over shell pattern
20 sts and 7 rows = 4" (10 cm) over yoke

❖ SKILLS USED

Chain (ch), p11; single crochet (sc), p13; double crochet (dc), p15; rejoining yarn, p39; shells and picots, p72–73

See pages 24–25 for pattern abbreviations.

LACY CAMISOLE

Note: The camisole is worked in one piece, with the edging and straps added. The cord is worked separately and is optional.

Using sport weight cotton and size D crochet hook, make a foundation chain of 217 sts, plus 2 turning ch.

Row 1: Skip 2 ch, 2 dc in next, [skip 2 ch, 1 sc, ch 5, skip 5 ch, 1 sc, skip 2 ch, 5 dc in next] 17 times, skip 2 ch, 1 sc, ch 5, skip 5 ch, 1 sc, skip 2 ch, 3 dc in last ch; turn.

Row 2: Ch 1 (does not count as sc), 1 sc in first st, [ch 5, 1 sc in 3rd of ch-5 loop, ch 5, 1 sc in 3rd of 5 dc] 17 times, ch 5, 1 sc in 3rd of ch-5 loop, ch 5, 1 sc in 3rd of ch-2 in previous row; turn.

Row 3: [Ch 5, 1 sc in ch loop, 5 dc in sc, 1 sc in ch loop] 18 times, ch 2, 1 dc in sc; turn.

Row 4: Ch 1 (does not count as sc), 1 sc in first st, [ch 5, 1 sc in 3rd of 5 dc, ch 5, 1 sc in 3rd of ch-5 loop] 18 times; turn.

Row 5: Ch 3, 2 dc in 1st st, [1 sc in ch loop, ch 5, 1 sc in ch loop, 5 dc in sc] 17 times; 1 sc in ch loop, ch 5, 1 sc in ch loop, 3 dc in last st.

Rows 2 to 5 form the shell pattern. Repeat these rows until work measures 9½" (24 cm).

Next row: Work 1 dc into each ch of previous row; skip each sc; 180 dc worked.

Next row: Work 1 dc into each dc of previous row.

Repeat last row 11 more times. Break off yarn.

BORDER AND STRAPS

Rejoin yarn to bottom corner of left front and work 81 sc, evenly spaced, up left front, then work 2 more sc in last st to turn corner. Work 26 sc, ch 80 (for left strap), skip 40 dc and rejoin with a sl st to next dc. Work 48 sc, ch 80 (for right strap), skip 40 dc and rejoin with a sl st to next dc. Work 26 sc. Work 2 more sc in last st to turn corner; then work 81 sc, evenly spaced, down right front; turn.

For the buttonholes; ch 2 (counts as 1st sc), [ch 2, skip 2 sts from previous row, 5 sc] 11 times, ch 2, skip 2 sts from previous row, 1 sc; work 2 more sc in last st to turn corner, then continue in sc around border to top of left edge and turn (do not work 2nd row of sc down left edge).

Next row (picot border): [Ch 4, sl st into same st, 2 sc] repeat across top, over left strap, across back, over right strap, along right top edge and down right-hand edge. Fasten off.

FINISHING

Sew buttons on left front to correspond with buttonholes.

DRAWSTRING

Make flat cord, 30" (76 cm) long (see pages 90–91). Weave it in and out of ch loops below bustline.

COLORWAYS

The choice of dusky pink yarn is fresh and feminine. But you could make this pretty top in any color—in primrose yellow for a sunny summer top, or in black yarn with contrasting red border for a really sophisticated effect.

FILET MESH

Fine yarns and narrow hooks can create delicate openwork fabric. Various techniques have evolved, which you can use to make a range of different patterns, all of which have a lacy look.

Filet crochet creates an open, lacy fabric. A series of squares forms a mesh. Patterns are made by leaving some squares of the mesh open (spaces) and filling others in (blocks). This technique can make geometric patterns and shapes like birds and flowers. Filet crochet is used for edgings as well as for tablecloths, curtains, and clothes.

CHARTS

Pattern instructions for filet crochet usually come on graph paper. Unless otherwise stated, read odd rows of a chart from right to left, even rows from left to right. You can usually adapt and use any squared chart as a pattern for filet work.

On filet charts, the spaces are represented by blank squares and the blocks by filled-in squares. The filet ground's vertical stitches are usually double crochet and the horizontal bars ch-2 spaces. Occasional special features called bars and lacets are drawn as they look.

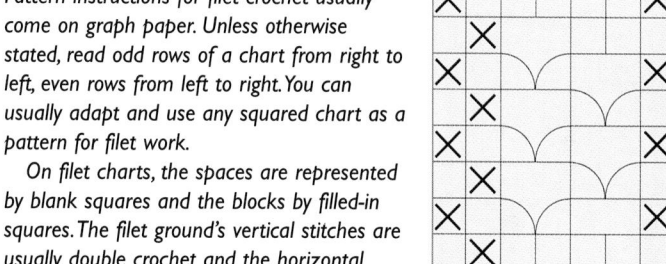

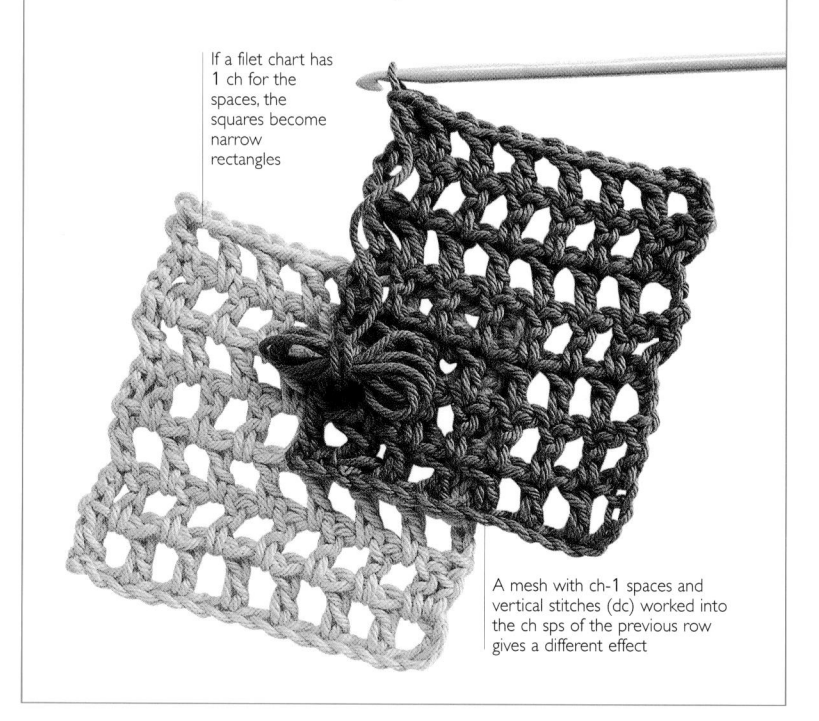

If a filet chart has 1 ch for the spaces, the squares become narrow rectangles

A mesh with ch-1 spaces and vertical stitches (dc) worked into the ch sps of the previous row gives a different effect

FILET MESH

To make a simple filet mesh of alternating blocks and spaces, first make a foundation chain: Make a multiple of 3 chain (ch) for each square required (which in turn will be a multiple of the number of squares in the pattern repeat), plus 1. Add 4 if the first square is a space, but only 2 if it is a block.

1 *To begin the first row with a space: Skip 7 ch, then work 1 double crochet (dc).*

2 *To begin the first row with a block: Skip 3 ch, then work 3 dc.*

3 *Thereafter, work each space as: Ch 2, skip 2, 1 dc. Work each block as: 3 dc.*

4 *From row 2, at the beginning of each row, ch 3 to count as the edge stitch (dc), skip the first dc, and then, for each space, ch 2, skip 2 ch (or next 2 dc of a block), 1 dc in next dc; and for each block, work 2 dc in ch-2 sp (or in next 2 dc of a block), 1 dc in next dc.*

BARS AND LACETS

A lacet is a variation of filet mesh. A bar is normally worked over the top of each lacet in the mesh. Each structure occupies 2 squares of the pattern and is usually worked alternately.

1 *To make a lacet: Ch 3, skip 2, 1 single crochet (sc), ch 3, skip 2, 1 dc.*

2 *To make a bar: Ch 5, skip lacet (or 2 squares), 1 dc.*

CLONES KNOTS

These knots can be used to embellish filet mesh. They are named for an Irish town that was an early center for lace making.

1 *To make the knot: Ch 3, *wrap yarn round hook (yo), take hook under ch loop just made, yo, bring hook back again over ch loop; repeat from * 4 more times (there are now 9 loops on the hook).*

2 *Yo and draw through all loops, slip stitch (sl st) in 1st of ch-3.*

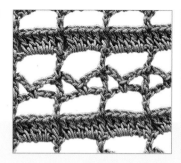

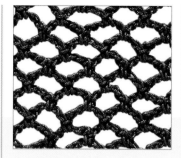

BLOCK, BAR, AND LACET
Multiple of 6 sts plus 1, plus 2 for foundation ch.

Row 1 (right side): Skip 3 ch, dc across, turn.

Row 2: Ch 3, skip first dc, *ch 5, skip 5, 1 dc; rep from * across, turn.

Row 3: Ch 3, skip first dc, *ch 3, 1 sc in ch loop, ch 3,—called lacet, 1 dc in dc; rep from * across, turn.

Row 4: Ch 3, skip first dc, *ch 5, skip lacet, 1 dc; rep from * across, turn.

Row 5: Ch 3, *5 dc in ch loop, 1 dc in dc; rep from * across, turn.

Rows 2 to 5 form the pattern.

BASIC TRELIS
Multiple of 4 sts plus 2, plus 4 for foundation ch.

Row 1 (right side): Skip 5 ch, 1 sc, *ch 5, skip 3 ch, 1 sc; rep from * across, turn.

Row 2: *Ch 5, 1 sc in 5 ch loop; rep from * across, turn.

Row 2 forms the pattern.

PUFF TRELIS
Multiple of 3 sts plus 1, plus 1 for foundation ch.

Special abbreviation puff V st: [Hdc3tog, ch 3, hdc3tog] in same place.

Row 1 (right side): Skip 1 ch, 1 sc, *ch 3, skip 2 ch, 1 sc; rep from * across, turn.

Row 2: Ch 4, 1 sc in ch loop, *ch 3, 1 sc in ch loop; rep from * across, ending ch 1, 1 dc in last st, turn.

Row 3: Ch 3,*1 puff V st in sc; rep from * across, ending 1 dc in t-ch loop, turn.

Rows 2 and 3 form the pattern.

SINGLE CROCHET NETWORK
Multiple of 8 sts plus 1, plus 1 for foundation ch.

Note: T-ch does not count as st, except on row 4, 10, etc.

Row 1 (right side): Skip 1 ch, 3 sc, *ch 5, skip 3 ch, 5 sc; rep from * across, omitting 2 of 5 sc at end of last rep, turn.

Row 2: Ch 1, 1 sc, *1 sc, ch 3, 1 sc in ch-5 loop, ch 3, skip 1 sc, 2 sc; rep from * across, turn.

Row 3: Ch 1, 1 sc, *ch 3, 1 sc in ch-3 sp, 1 sc, 1 sc in ch-3 sp, ch 3, skip 1 sc, 1 sc; rep from * across, turn.

Row 4: Ch 5 (counts as 1 dc and 2 ch), * 1 sc in ch-3 sp, 3 sc, 1 sc in ch-3 sp **, ch 5; rep from * to 2nd last ch-3 sp and from * to ** again, ch 2, 1 dc in last sc, turn.

Row 5: Ch 1, 1 sc, *ch 3, skip 1 sc, 3 sc, ch 3, skip 1 sc, 1 sc in ch-5 loop; rep from * across, turn.

Row 6: Ch 1, 1 sc, *1 sc in ch-3 sp, ch 3, skip 1 sc, 1 sc, ch 3, skip 1 sc, 1 sc in ch-3 sp, 1 sc; rep from * across, turn.

Row 7: Ch 1, 1 sc, *1 sc, 1 sc in ch-3 sp, ch 5, 1 sc in ch-3 sp, 2 sc; rep from * across, turn.

Rows 2 to 7 form the pattern.

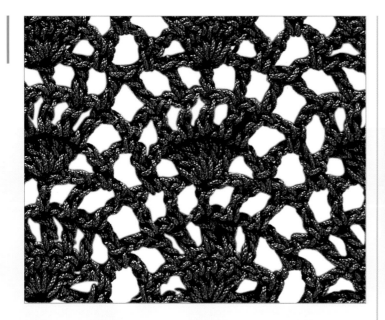

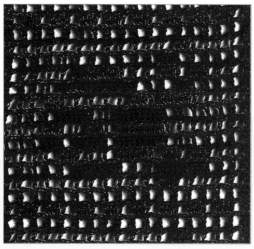

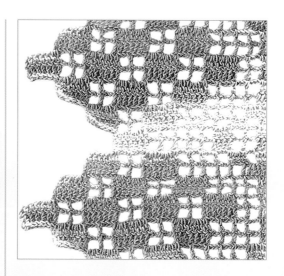

FOUNTAIN NETWORK

Multiple of 12 sts plus 5, plus 1 for foundation ch.

Row 1 (right side): Skip 1 ch, 1 sc, *ch 5, skip 3 ch, 1 sc, ch 2, skip 3 ch, 5 dc in next, ch 2, skip 3 ch, 1 sc; rep from * to last 4 ch, ch 5, skip 3 ch, 1 sc, turn.

Row 2: Ch 5 (counts as 1 dc and 2 ch), *1 sc in ch-5 loop, ch 2, skip 2 ch, 1 dc in dc, [ch 1, 1 dc] 4 times, ch 2, skip 2 ch; rep from * to last ch-5 loop, 1 sc in ch-5 loop, ch 2, 1 dc in sc, turn.

Row 3: Ch 4 (counts as 1 dc and 1 ch), 1 dc in first st, *skip [2 ch, 1 sc, 2 ch], 1 dc in dc, [ch 2, skip

1 ch, 1 dc] 4 times; rep from * ending skip [2 ch, 1 sc, 2 ch], [1 dc, ch 1, 1 dc] in t-ch loop, turn.

Row 4: Ch 1 (does not count as sc), 1 sc, skip [1 ch, 2 dc], *ch 5, 1 sc in ch-2 sp, ch 2, skip [1 dc, 2 ch], 5 dc in dc, ch 2, skip [2 ch, 1 dc], 1 sc in ch-2 sp; rep from * ending ch 5, 1 sc in t-ch loop, turn.

Rows 2, 3, and 4 form the pattern.

FILET ROSE INSERTION

Foundation: Ch 60.

Row 1 (right side): Skip 3 ch, 3 dc, [ch 2, skip 2, 1 dc] 17 times, 3 dc, turn (19 squares).

Follow chart from row 2 for pattern, repeating rows 3 to 16 as required.

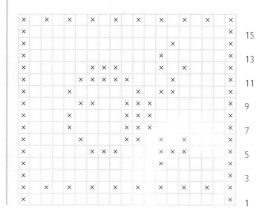

FILET DIAMOND BORDER

Foundation: Ch 36.

Note: For multiple increases and decreases see pages 20 to 23.

Row 1 (right side): Skip 3 ch, 3 dc, [ch 2, skip 2, 1 dc] twice, 3 dc [ch 2, skip 2, 1 dc] 5 times, [3 dc] twice, turn.

Follow chart from row 2 for pattern, repeating rows 2 to 12 as required.

MESH COVER-UP

Seamless and lightweight, this pullover can be slipped on over a bikini or strap top. It is shown in a yarn that looks like denim and goes great with jeans.

❖ SIZE
One size: To fit 34–36" (86–91 cm) bust. Finished size 37½" (95 cm) around bust and 20" (50 cm) from shoulder to hem.

❖ MATERIALS
Yarn *Denim-look knitting worsted 100% cotton, 8 x 50 g balls*
Hooks *One size F crochet hook*
Notions *Tapestry needle*

❖ GAUGE
9 loops and 18 rows = 8" (20 cm) over trellis pattern 19 sts = 4" (10 cm) over hem

❖ SKILLS USED
Chain (ch), p11; single crochet (sc), p13; joining seams, p27; rejoining yarn, p39; working in the round, p53; basic trellis pattern, p78

See pages 24–25 for pattern abbreviations.

MESH COVER-UP

Note: The sweater is worked in one piece, in the round, starting with the lower edge, so back and front are worked together.

Using cotton yarn and size F hook, ch 212, join with sl st in first ch to form ring.
Round 1: Ch 2, sc in each ch.
Repeat round **1** two more times.
Round 4: Ch 5, skip 3, *1 sc, ch 5, skip 3, rep from * to end; join with a sc in first ch loop.
Round 5: *Ch 5, 1 sc in ch loop, rep from * to last loop; ch 5 and join with a sc in first ch loop.
Round 5 forms the basic trellis pattern. Repeat this 28 more times.

ALTERNATIVE IDEAS

Instead of adding sleeves, you could make a vest. Simply complete the main part of garment and join at the shoulders. Leave it as it is or work a single row of sc around the armholes for a neat finish.

 To make a longer or shorter sweater, simply work more or fewer rounds before shaping the back and front.

YARN AND COLOR IDEAS

Make this pullover in a gold or silver glittery yarn for an evening cover-up to wear over a strappy dress or a skimpy top and trousers. Or make it in a bright cotton for beach wear over a swimming suit or bikini.

To shape the back, work 17 loops in basic trellis pattern and turn; **work 4 more rows of 17 loops.
Next row: Ch 5, sc in next ch loop; *ch 4, sc in next ch loop, rep from * until last loop; ch 5, sc in loop; turn; work 2 more rows like this.
Next row: Ch 5, sc in next ch loop; *ch 3, sc in next ch loop, rep from * until last loop; ch 5, sc in loop; turn; work 2 more rows like this.
Next row: Ch 5, sc in next ch loop; *ch 2, sc in next ch loop, rep from * until last loop; ch 5, sc in loop; turn; work 2 more rows like this. Fasten off yarn.
To shape the front, count 4 loops from beginning of back shaping and rejoin yarn; work 17 loops in basic trellis pattern and turn, then proceed from ** in exactly the same way as back.

SLEEVES

Using a tapestry needle and length of yarn, stitch the front and back together at shoulders. Rejoin yarn at one shoulder and work in basic trellis pattern around armhole (ch 5, 1 sc in each ch loop); 20 loops.
To shape sleeve, working from shoulder to wrist in rounds: Work 9 rounds of ch 5, 1 sc; 10 rounds of ch 4, 1 sc; 22 rounds of ch 3, 1 sc; 10 rounds of ch 2, 1 sc; 2 rounds of ch 1, 1 sc. Fasten off yarn.
Repeat for second sleeve.

Note: Some denim-look yarns can shrink after the first wash, making the garment shorter in length. The color will also fade after washing.

AFGHAN STITCH

Afghan stitch (sometimes called Tunisian crochet) is worked with a special

hook that is longer than usual, has a uniform diameter, and has a knob (or

sometimes another hook) at the other end.

FINISHING TECHNIQUES

When you've finished a piece of Afghan stitch, you may find that the edges curl. To combat this you need to block and press your work. Lay the piece out flat, wrong side up, on a padded surface. Smooth it out and pin around the edges, making sure you don't stretch the work out of shape. Cover the piece with a damp cloth and press lightly, with the iron on a warm setting. Alternatively, hold a steaming iron close to the surface, but not actually touching.

The Afghan stitch technique is a cross between knitting and crochet. The finished work resembles knitting, but the stitches are thicker and firmer. Plain, textured, multicolored, and openwork patterns are possible.

For Afghan stitch, you will use a hook at least two sizes larger than you would ordinarily use with the same yarn in regular crochet. Unless a double-ended hook is used, the work is never turned and so the right side is always facing.

The odd-numbered rows are worked from right to left, as loops are picked up and retained on the hook. In the even-numbered rows, the loops are worked off again from left to right.

Afghan crochet is ideal when you want to create something that's sturdy and hardwearing, like this shoulder bag (see page 84).

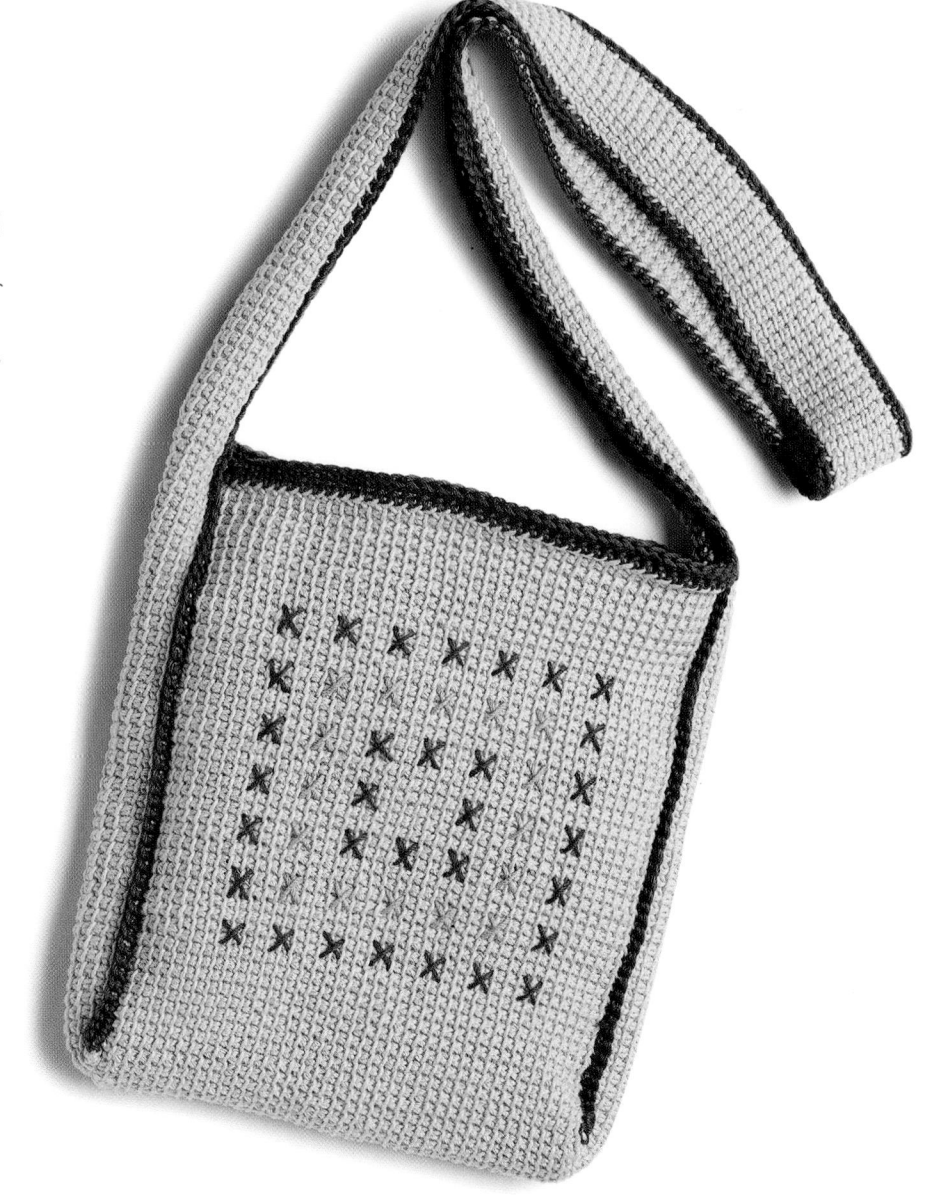

FOUNDATION ROW

You should make a foundation chain with the same number of chains as the number of stitches required in the finished row, plus 1 chain for turning.

1 *To make row one (forward row): Make a foundation chain. Skip 1 chain (ch), *insert the hook in the next ch, wrap the yarn round the hook (yo), draw the loop through the ch only and keep the loop on the hook.*

2 *Repeat from * across. Do not turn the work at the end.*

3 *To make row two (return row): Yo, draw through 1 loop only, *yo, draw through 2 loops; rep from * across until 1 loop remains on the hook. Do not turn the work at the end.*

4 *These two rows make the finished foundation row—the basis of most Afghan stitch patterns.*

SIMPLE AFGHAN STITCH

Work the basic forward and return foundation row.

*Forward (row 3 and all odd rows): Count loop on hook as first st and start in 2nd stitch (st). *Insert hook at front and from right to left around single front vertical yarn, yo, draw through and keep on hook; rep from * across. Do not turn.*

Return (even rows): Same as row two (return row).

AFGHAN STOCKINETTE STITCH

Work the basic forward and return foundation row.

*Forward (row 3 and all odd rows): Count loop on hook as first st and start in 2nd st. *Insert hook from front through fabric and below chs formed by previous return row to right of front vertical yarn and left of back yarn of same loop, yo, draw loop through and keep on hook; rep from * across. Do not turn.*

Return: (even rows): Same as row two (return row).

HARDWORKING SHOULDER BAG

If you put your bags to the test, try this sturdy pattern made with the Afghan crochet stitch. The bag is cleverly embellished with rows of cross-stitched Xs.

❖ **SIZE**
One size: 6¾" (17 cm) wide, 8" (20 cm) long and 1⅜" (3.5 cm) deep

❖ **MATERIALS**
Yarn Cotton glacé 100% cotton, 2 x 50 g balls in color A, 1 x 50 g ball contrasting color B (for border and embroidery), small amounts of contrasting color C (for embroidery)
Hook One size 4 Afghan crochet hook
Notions Tapestry needle

❖ **GAUGE**
24 sts and 24 rows = 4" (10 cm)

❖ **SKILLS USED**
Chain (ch), p11; slip stitch (sl st), p11; single crochet (sc), p13; joining seams, p27; changing colors, p39; simple Afghan stitch, p83

See pages 24–25 for pattern abbreviations.

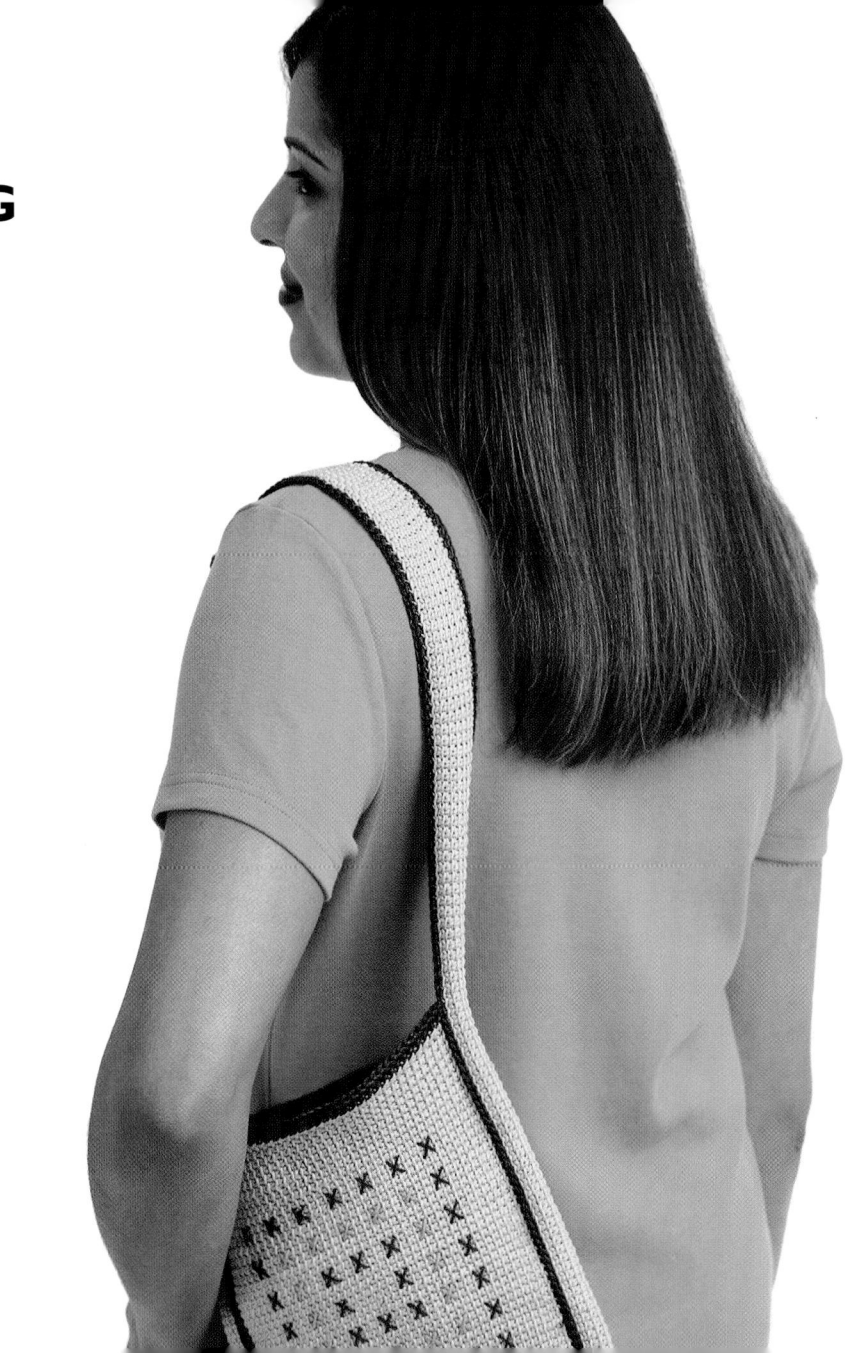

SHOULDER BAG

Using color A and size 4 Afghan crochet hook, ch 45.

Row 1: Skip 1 ch, (insert hook in next ch, yo, draw loop through ch only and keep on hook) repeat to end. Do not turn.

Row 2 (and all even rows): Yo, draw through 1 loop, *yo, draw through 2 loops, repeat from * until 1 loop remains on hook. Do not turn.

Row 3 (and all odd rows): Count loop on hook as first st and start in second st. *Insert hook at front and from right to left around single front vertical thread, yo, draw through and keep on hook, repeat from * across. Do not turn.

Work a total of 98 rows. Break off yarn

GUSSET AND STRAP

Along one side of work, count in 45 rows from each end. Loop the center 8 sts onto hook then starting with Row 2 of Afghan simple stitch, work until you have completed 255 rows. Join with sl sts to the central 8 rows on the opposite side.

EMBROIDERY

Using the chart as a guide, stitch the design at the center of the back and front of the bag. Use colors B and C, as indicated on the chart, threaded into a tapestry needle. Each square on the grid corresponds to one crochet stitch. Each cross stitch (see below) is worked over four crochet stitches (two rows of two stitches). This is also the size of the gap between each cross stitch.

JOINING AND EDGING

Using color B, work two rows of sc on the two top edges of the bag. Then, starting at one of the lower corners of the bag and matching row for row, join the edge of the strap (which will form the gusset) to the edge of the bag, with a row of sc. When you reach the top of the bag, carry on in sc along the edge of the strap until you come to the opposite top edge, then continue as before, joining the edge of the strap to the edge of the bag. Repeat for the other side of the bag.

JOINING TIPS

The edge formed by this pattern is very firm and it is easy to match the ends of rows when joining. You may find it easier to pin the edge of the strap to the edge of the bag before you start to join them with a row of single crochet. Just remove each pin as you get to it.

CROSS STITCH

To make a cross stitch, bring the needle out at the top left of the four stitches you are going to cover. Insert it again at bottom right. Bring the needle out again at bottom left and insert again at top right to finish the stitch. Repeat, following the chart as a guide and changing color as indicated.

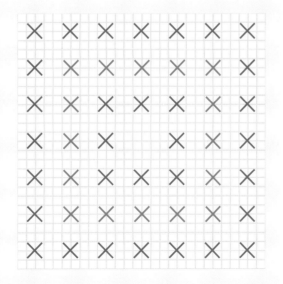

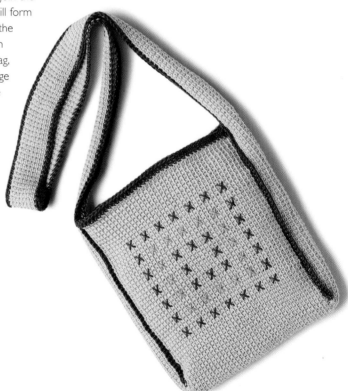

EDGINGS

Many crocheted items benefit from a special edge or border. They not only

add interest, but give a better finish and help the crochet lie flat.

If an edging or border is to be the foundation for your main piece, make it first. If you are going to attach an edging afterward, make it separately. When working an edging, use a smaller size hook than you used for the main piece. This will give the edging a firmer finish.

To make an edging, normally you work one stitch into each stitch across the top of a row and into the underside of a foundation chain. When you get to a corner, you work three stitches into the corner and along the side of the fabric at the rate of one stitch per single crochet row. As a guide, you will need to use one and two stitches alternately per half double crochet row, two stitches per double crochet row, three stitches per triple row, etc.

MAKING A CORDED EDGE

*Working from left to right, insert the hook into the next stitch to the right, wrap the yarn round the hook (yo). Draw the loop through the work, below the loop which remains on the hook, and up to the left, into the normal working position (left). Yo and draw the loop through to complete 1 corded single crochet (right). Repeat from *.

SINGLE-CROCHET EDGING

This basic edging, worked with the right side facing, neatens and strengthens the fabric and can cover any float yarns or stray short ends. It is also a good foundation for a more decorative edging.

BUTTONHOLE LOOPS

Loops for buttons may be made in an edging row by skipping the required number of stitches and working chains instead. If you need extra edging rows, work sc into the loops.

CORDED EDGE

This is a very effective edging, usually worked after one round of sc and with the right side facing. Work it in sc, but from left to right. (See below left.)

PICOT EDGING

Picots of varying size and complexity are a regular feature of crochet edgings. To make a simple picot, see page 73. For more complex designs, see page 87.

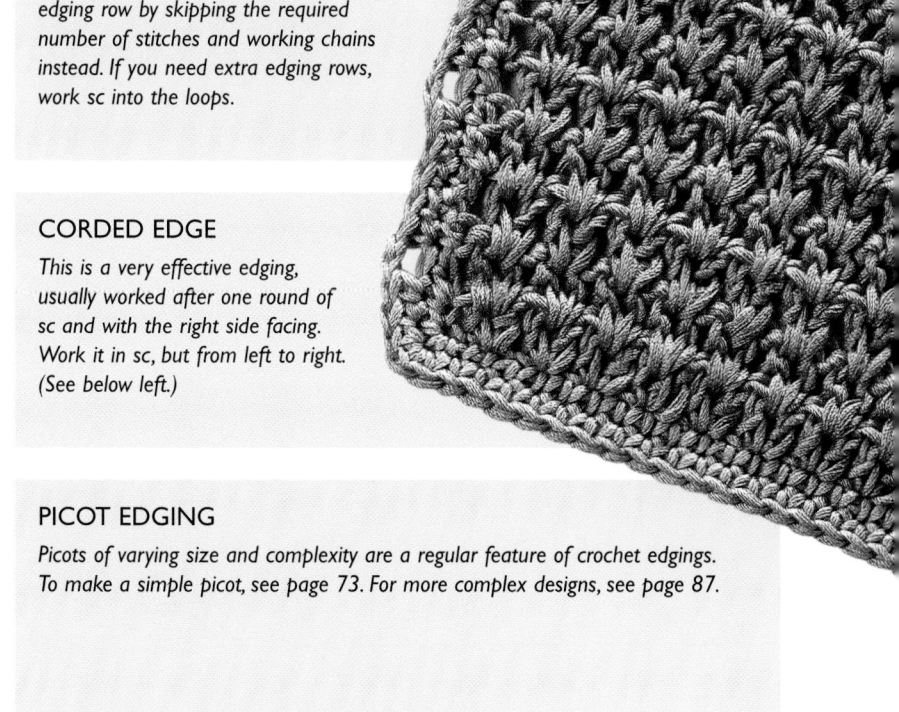

PICOT ARCHWAY

Multiple of 8 sts plus 1, plus 1 for foundation ch.

Row 1 (right side): Skip 2 ch, sc across, turn.

Row 2: Ch 1, sc across, turn.

Row 3: Ch 1 (does not count as sc), 1 sc, *ch 3, 2 dc in next, skip 2, 1 sc; rep from * across, turn.

Row 4: Ch 4 (counts as 1 dc, ch 1), 1 dc in first, * 1 sc in ch-3 loop, ch 6, 1 sc in ch-3 loop, (1 dc, ch 3, 1 dc—called V st) in sc; rep from * omitting 2 of 3 ch in last V st, turn.

Row 5: Ch 1, 1 sc in ch-1 sp, *[5 dc, ch 5, sl st in 5th ch from hook, 5 dc] in ch-6 loop, 1 sc in next ch loop; rep from * across.

BULLION SPIRALS

Foundation: Ch 12.

Special abbreviation bst (bullion stitch): Made with (yo) 10 times (see page 67).

Row 1 (right side): Skip 3 ch, 1 dc, skip 3 ch, (1 dc, [1 bst, 1 dc] 3 times—called shell) in next, skip 3 ch, (3 dc, ch 2, 3 dc—called V st) in next, turn.

Row 2: Ch 7, skip 3 ch, [3 dc in next] 4 times, V st in ch-2 sp, ch 3, 1 sc in center bst of shell, ch 3, 1 dc in each of last 2 sts, turn.

Row 3: Ch 3, 1 dc, skip 3 ch, shell in sc, skip 3 ch, V st in ch-2 sp, turn.

Rows 2 and 3 form the pattern.

PICOT SCALLOPS

Multiple of 8 sts plus 1, plus 2 for foundation ch.

Row 1 (right side): Skip 3 ch, 1 dc, *ch 1, skip 1, 1 dc; rep from * to last ch, 1 dc, turn.

Row 2: Ch 5 (counts as 1 dc, ch 2), dc2tog in first, *skip [1 dc, 1 ch], 3 dc, skip [1 ch, 1 dc], [dc2tog, ch 4, dc2tog—called 2cl] in ch sp; rep from * across, omitting last 2 ch and dc2tog from last 2cl and working 1 dc in same loop, turn.

Row 3: Ch 3 (counts as 1 hdc, ch 1), 1 sc in ch-2 sp, *skip cl, [ch 3, 1 sc—called pc], skip 1, 1 pc, 2 pc in ch-4 loop; rep from * across, omiting 2nd pc at end of last rep and working ch 1, 1 hdc in same loop, turn.

Row 4: Ch 1 (does not count as sc), 1 sc, *ch 1, skip 1 pc, [dc2tog, (ch 3, dc2tog) twice] in next pc, ch 1, skip 1 pc, 1 sc in next pc; rep from * across, turn.

Row 5: Ch 1 (does not count as sc), 1 sc, skip 1 ch, *[2 pc in next ch-3 loop] twice, skip 1 ch, 1 pc in sc; rep from * across.

TRIPLE PICOT

Multiple of 5 sts.

Note: All rows worked right side facing.

Row 1: With yarn matching main fabric, sc.

Row 2: With contrasting color, *5 sc, [ch 3, sl st in 3rd ch from hook] 3 times, sl st in top of last sc made; rep from *.

(Main fabric represented here by a row of dc.)

LACE TRIM

Transform a plain sweater you buy or knit into something special with the addition of a narrow velvet ribbon and a length of sumptuous hand-crocheted lace.

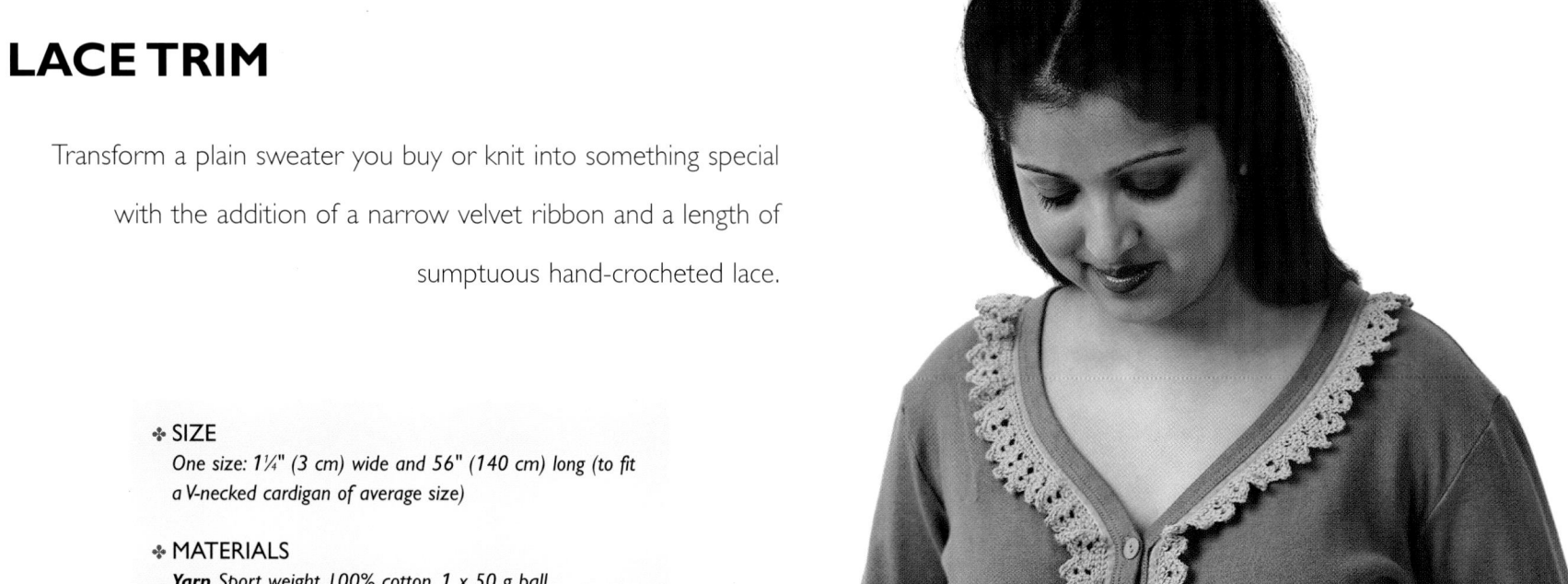

❖ SIZE
   One size: 1¼" (3 cm) wide and 56" (140 cm) long (to fit a V-necked cardigan of average size)

❖ MATERIALS
   Yarn *Sport weight 100% cotton, 1 x 50 g ball*
   Hook *One size F crochet hook*
   Notions *57¼" (143 cm) of narrow velvet ribbon, sewing needle and thread to match ribbon and crochet trim*

❖ GAUGE
   27 sc = 4" (10 cm) (first row)
   4 rows = 1¼" (3 cm)

❖ SKILLS USED
   Chain (ch), p11; single crochet (sc), p13; edgings, p86

See page 24–25 for pattern abbreviations.

LACE TRIM

Using 4 ply cotton and size F hook, ch 379; turn.

Row 1: Skip 2 ch, continue in sc to end of row.

Row 2: Ch 2, 1 sc *ch 3, skip 1, 3 sc, rep from * to last 3 sts; ch 3, skip 1, 2 sc; turn.

Row 3: Ch 2, *skip 1, (2 sc, ch 3, 2 sc) in ch-3 loop, skip 1, 1 sc, rep from * to end; turn.

Row 4: Ch 2, *(3 sc, ch 3, 3 sc) in ch-3 loop, 1 sc in sc of previous row, rep from * to end.

FINISHING

Stitch the narrow ribbon to the edge of the button band on the cardigan, turning each raw end under ⅝" (1.5 cm). Pin the crochet trim in place. Pin the two ends to the two lower edges of the cardigan fronts, then pin the center of the trim to the center of the back neck edge. Then pin along the rest of the trim. Stitch in place.

SIZE GUIDE

The finished length of this lacy trim is 56" (140 cm), made on a foundation chain of 379. If you want to make a longer or shorter length of trim, the foundation chain should be a multiple of 4 sts, plus 5, plus 2 for a turning chain.

If you find that it is slightly too long, ease in the extra as you pin it in place. This will give a slightly gathered appearance. If, however, you find that your finished work is too short, do not stretch it to fit as it will only shrink back to its original size when the garment is washed.

CORDS AND FINISHING TOUCHES

Crocheted buttons and cords will liven up accessories such as bags. Adding surface chains to a piece of finished crochet creates a decorative effect somewhat like weaving.

ALTERNATIVE IDEAS

You can use handmade cords for other handcrafted items—they are just as useful when teamed with knitted or sewn items. Use remnants of yarn to make cords for drawstring bags.

You might also want to experiment with alternatives to crochet cord. Ribbons, in varying thicknesses, can look very pretty threaded through crochet work. Or use purchased decorative cord in contrasting colors.

You can use ordinary buttons on your crochet, but chunky crochet buttons are easy to make and offer a colorful, lively way of enhancing both knitted and crocheted garments and accessories. For a crochet buttonhole loop, see page 86.

Handmade cords are also useful—they can be used as ties and drawstrings to fasten openings in bags and garments. Both flat and round cords can be worked quickly and easily. Made in contrasting colors, they can add bright and decorative touches to crochet or knitted garments and accessories.

Surface chains are a way to apply additional pattern. Plaids need careful planning, but any crocheted design, particularly one with a network of chain spaces, may be decorated in this way with vertical or horizontal lines.

Made in the same dyed yarn as the bag, this rainbow-like cord is the perfect finishing touch (see page 58).

BOBBLE BUTTON

This is worked in the round. Make a foundation chain: Chain (ch) 2. Close this and each subsequent round with a slip stitch (sl st) in first single crochet (sc). Round 1 (right side): 6 sc in 2nd ch from hook. Round 2: Ch 1, 2 sc in each sc (12 stitches (sts)). Round 3: Ch 1, 1 sc in each sc (left). Round 4: Ch 1, (1 sc, skip 1) 6 times (6 sts). Pack the button with a small amount of yarn (right). Round 5: Ch 1, (1 sc, skip 1) 3 times. Cut a length of yarn to close the opening and sew the button in place.

ROUND CORD

Make a foundation ring: Ch 5 (or as required for thickness of cord). Work in a spiral around the ring as follows: 1 sl st in top loop of each ch and then of each sl st, until cord reaches required length. For a faster-growing cord, work in sc or double crochet (dc).

FLAT CORD

Ch 2, 1 sc in 2nd ch from hook, turn and work 1 sc in ch at back of sc just made, *turn and work 1 sc, inserting hook down through 2 loops at back of sc just made; rep from * until cord is required length.

MAKING SURFACE CHAINS

1. Make a slip knot in new yarn. With right or wrong side facing as required, insert hook down through chosen chain space. Yo underneath work, draw through work and loop on hook.

2. *Insert hook down through next chain space or selected position, yo underneath fabric, draw through fabric and loop on hook; rep from * as required. Make one chain beyond edge of work and fasten off. It is important to work loosely so as not to distort the background stitches. It may help to use a larger hook than you used for the main work. Short ends of yarn should be worked over and encased during any subsequent edging rounds or darned into the wrong side of the piece.

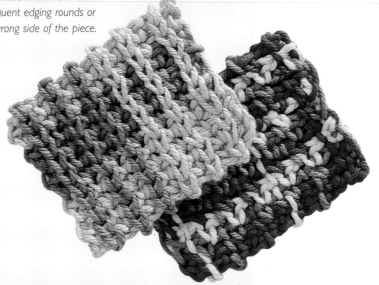

FUNKY FLOWERS

Make a whole bunch of flowers, in different colorways, to make the perfect finishing touch for lapels, hats, sweaters, chokers, and wristbands.

❖ SIZE
One size: Flower is 3" (7.5 cm) wide. Leaf is 2¼" (6 cm) long and 1½" (4 cm) wide.

❖ MATERIALS
Yarn *Small amounts of cotton glacé in color A (for flower) and color B (for leaves)*
Hook *One size C hook*
Notions *Tapestry needle, pearl button*

❖ GAUGE
Each flower measures 3" (7.5 cm) across.

❖ SKILLS USED
Chain (ch), p11; slip stitch (sl sp), p11; single crochet (sc), p13; double crochet (dc), p15; triple crochet (tr), p15; changing colors, p39; working in the round, p53

See page 24–25 for pattern abbreviations.

FUNKY FLOWERS

Each flower is made in two parts: An outer set of petals and a smaller center.

OUTER PETALS

Using cotton glacé in color A and size C hook, ch 9, join with a sl st in first ch to form foundation ring.

Round 1: Ch 3, 2 dc into ring, (ch 6, sl st sideways into top of last dc, 3 dc in ring) 5 times, ch 6, sl st sideways into top of last dc, sl st in 3rd ch of ch-3.

Round 2: Sl st into first dc of previous round, (11 dc into ch-6 loop, sl st in center dc of 3 dc group) 5 times, 11 dc into ch-6 loop, sl st to first sl st. Fasten off.

TIPS AND HINTS

As with all small-scale crochet projects, this is an ideal way to use up scraps from larger projects. Use your own color combinations: you could make the inner and outer parts of the flower from different colors. You could also try a fancy button for the middle of your flower.

CENTER PETALS

Make a foundation ring of 9 ch, as before, and work round **1** only; fasten off.

LEAF

Using cotton glacé in color B and size C hook, ch 10; turn.

Row 1: 1 sl st into each of first 3 ch; 1 sc into each of next 3 ch; 1 dc into each of next 3 ch; 5 tr into last ch. Now work back down the other side of the foundation ch: 1 dc into each of next 3 ch; 1 sc into each of next 3 ch; 1 sl st into each of last 3 ch.

Row 2: 1 sl st into each of first 3 sts; 1 sc into each of next 3 sts; 1 dc into each of next 3 sts; 1 tr into each of next 2 sts; 3 tr into next st; 1 tr into each of next 2 st;) 1 dc into each of next 3 sts; 1 sc into each of next 3 sts; 1 sl st into each of last 3 sts. Fasten off. Make more leaves, as required.

FINISHING

Stitch the outer and center petals together and stitch a button over the hole in the center. Stitch a leaf or leaves to the back of the flower, attaching the pointed ends to the center back of the flower.

DYEING YARNS

Although store-bought yarns come in a wide range of colors, you might want to try something a little different. Experiment with dyeing yarns and you can guarantee your finished crochet will be unique.

Start with white 100 per cent cotton yarn. Use cold water dyes and be careful to follow the manufacturer's instructions to ensure the dyed yarn remains colorfast—in other words, the color will not run when you wash the finished garment. Wear rubber gloves when handling the dyes to protect your hands.

DYEING YARNS

Yarn is sometimes available in hanks. If, however, you are starting with a ball of yarn, you will need to unwind it and then rewind it into a loose hank. Tie the hank loosely with short lengths of yarn in two or three places.

Wash the hank of yarn in soapy water then rinse thoroughly in several changes of clean water. Wring out excess water and leave damp.

Dissolve the dye powder and mix with water, soda, and salt, according to the manufacturer's instructions (top). Pour each color into a separate bucket or deep bowl. For this yarn, three different colors have been used.

Immerse a portion of the hank into one of the buckets of dye. In the middle photograph, about half the yarn in immersed in yellow dye. Place a wooden spoon or stick across the top of the bucket, to support the yarn and keep the undyed part out of the dye. You will need to leave the yarn immersed in the dye for about 1 hour.

Remove the yarn from the dye and squeeze out excess. Then immerse another portion of the hank in another color—in the bottom photograph, a quarter of the yarn is dipped in blue dye. Then repeat with a third color until the desired result has been achieved.

Wash the dyed yarn in soapy water and rinse thoroughly, then leave to dry before winding into a ball. The dyed yarn is then ready to use.

Simple sash belt
Rowan Summer Tweed
Exotic #512

String bikini top
Rowan Cotton Glacé
Pier #809

Peek-a-boo pillow cover
Rowan Handknit Knitting Worsted
Cotton
Color A Chime #204
Color B Flame #254

Striped halter top
Rowan Lurex Shimmer
Color A Minty #337
Color B Bedazzled #338

Zigzag scarf
Debbie Bliss Merino Knitting
Worsted
Color A #605
Color B #607

Twenty-squares throw
Jaeger Matchmaker Merino Aran
Color A Pink #773
Color B Charcoal gray #639

Bucket hats
Adult hat
Rowan Cotton Glacé
Sunny #802

Baby hat
Rowan Sport Weight Cotton
Cheeky #133

Multicolored bag
12-gauge cotton yarn, dyed to
shade required

Beaded bag
Rowan Sport Weight Cotton
Ripple #121

Tubular tote
Rowan Cotton Glacé
Color A Sky #749
Color B Splendour #810
Color C Bleached #726

Pet basket with liner
Utility string

Granny square top
Rowan Sport Weight Cotton
Color A Zest #134
Color B Cheeky #133
Color C Fennel #135
Rowan Cotton Glacé
Color D Splendour #810

Bobble hat
Rowan Yorkshire Tweed Knitting
Worsted
Revel #342

Lacy camisole
Rowan Sport Weight Cotton
Orchid #120

Mesh cover-up
Rowan Denim
Memphis #229

Hardworking shoulder bag
Rowan Cotton Glacé
Color A Zeal #813
Color B Mystic #808
Color C Shoot #814

Lace trim
Rowan Sport Weight Cotton
Bluebell #136

Funky flowers
Rowan Cotton Glacé
Color A Tickle #811
Color B Shoot #814

ACKNOWLEDGMENTS
The author would like to thank Rowan Yarns for all their help in supplying yarns for this book.

Carroll and Brown would like to thank The Mayhew Animal Home (www.mayhewanimalhome.org) for their assistance with this project.

Production Karol Davies
IT Paul Stradling
Photographic Assistant David Yems

SUPPLIERS

Rowan (USA)
4 Townsend West, Suite 8,
Nashua, New Hampshire
03064 USA
Tel (603) 886 5041/5043
wfibers@aol.com